THE APOSTLE PAUL

THE TEACHER, PREACHER, APOLOGIST

EDWARD D. ANDREWS

THE APOSTLE PAUL

What Made the Apostle Paul's Teachings, Preaching, Evangelism, and Apologetics Outstandingly Effective?

Edward D. Andrews

Christian Publishing House
Cambridge, Ohio

Copyright © 2018, 2024 Edward D. Andrews

All rights reserved. Except for brief quotations in articles, other publications, book reviews, and blogs, no part of this book may be reproduced in any manner without prior written permission from the publishers. For information, write, support@christianpublishers.org

THE APOSTLE PAUL: What Made the Apostle Paul's Teachings, Preaching, Evangelism, and Apologetics Outstandingly Effective? by Edward D. Andrews

ISBN-13: 978-1-949586-03-9

ISBN-10: 1-949586-03-0

Table of Contents

Book Description 12
Preface 14
Introduction 16
Chapter 1: Gamaliel Taught Saul of Tarsus 19
    Just Who Was Gamaliel? 19
    How Was Paul Taught by Gamaliel? 21
    The Teachings of Gamaliel 23
    What Did It Mean for Paul? 24
Chapter 2: Why Paul? 27
    Paul's Background and Conversion 27
    The Unique Qualifications of Paul 28
    Paul's Theological Contributions 28
    Paul's Missionary Journeys 29
    The Enduring Legacy of Paul 29
Chapter 3: Why You? 31
    Paul's Conversion and Early Life 31
    Unique Qualifications for Apostleship 31
    Theological Contributions 32
    Evangelistic Strategies 32
    Paul's Endurance and Commitment 33
Chapter 4: Paul's Effective Strategies of Teaching 35
    Paul's Methods of Teaching 35
    Teaching, Preaching, Evangelism, and Apologetics 35
    Examples of Paul's Boldness in Teaching 35
    Simplicity and Clarity in Teaching 36
    Use of Questions in Teaching 36

    Active Listening and Respect for Others..................................36

    Irrefutable Logic and Use of Scripture......................................36

    Hyperbole in Teaching...37

    Collaborative Teaching and Mentoring.....................................37

    Applying Paul's Strategies Today 37

Chapter 5: Teach with Insight and Persuasiveness 38

    The Importance of Being a Good Listener................................38

    Using Questions to Dig Deeper..38

    Understanding How Unbelievers Hear Christians....................39

    Effective Listening and Responding...39

    Speaking with Purpose..39

    The Value of Simplicity...40

    Effective Use of Questions 40

    Explaining and Proving 40

Chapter 6: Overcoming the Weaknesses in Our Teaching 42

    Recognizing Weaknesses 42

    Preparation and Study...42

    Understanding the Audience..42

    Effective Communication 43

    Addressing Misunderstandings..43

    Utilizing Questions 43

    Simplifying Complex Concepts 43

    Engaging Through Narrative 44

    Encouragement and Exhortation...44

    Being Adaptive and Flexible 44

    Practical Application...44

    Building Confidence in the Message...45

Chapter 7: Paul's Use of Secular Knowledge to Defend the Faith 46

Engaging with Cultural Contexts 46

Utilizing Philosophical Reasoning 46

Addressing Different Worldviews 47

Quoting Secular Sources 47

Integrating Historical Context 47

Practical Application for Modern Christians 47

Developing Intellectual Rigor 48

Balancing Faith and Reason 48

Emphasizing the Power of the Gospel 48

Chapter 8: Use Persuasion to Help Others to Accept Jesus Christ & Defend Your Faith 50

Paul Before Agrippa and Bernice 50

Paul's Defense Before Agrippa 50

Paul's Explanation of His Conversion 51

Festus' and Agrippa's Responses 51

Using the Art of Persuasion 52

Persuasion That Appeals to the Heart 52

Using the Word of God Skillfully 53

Have God's View of Christian Apologetic Evangelism ... 53

How to Be Successful in Sharing God's Word 53

Chapter 9: Paul's Letter to Philemon 55

Context and Purpose 55

Opening Greetings 55

Thanksgiving and Prayer 55

Appeal for Onesimus 56

Transformation of Onesimus 56

Request for Reconciliation 56
Paul's Offer to Repay 57
Closing Remarks and Benediction 57

Chapter 10: Paul's Theology of Suffering and Perseverance 58

The Nature of Christian Suffering 58
Identifying with Christ in Suffering 58
The Redemptive Value of Suffering 59
Perseverance Through Faith 59
The Role of Prayer and the Word 59
Community Support 60
The Example of Paul's Own Suffering 60
The Ultimate Hope 60

Chapter 11: Paul's Vision of Unity in the Body of Christ ... 62

The Basis of Unity in Christ 62
Unity in the Body of Christ 63
The Call to Live in Harmony 63
Overcoming Divisions 64
Practical Steps for Unity 64
Unity in Worship and Service 64
The Example of Christ 65
The Witness of Unity 65

Chapter 12: Paul's Mentorship of Timothy 67

Meeting Timothy 67
Timothy's Background and Faith 67
Training and Mentoring 68
Paul's Instructions to Timothy 68
Preparing Timothy for Leadership 69

Encouragement and Support..69

The Legacy of Paul's Mentorship 70

Chapter 13: Paul and His Many Traveling Companions....71

Barnabas: The Encourager...71

Silas: The Faithful Partner...71

Timothy: The Loyal Disciple 72

Luke: The Beloved Physician 72

Titus: The Trusted Delegate 73

Priscilla and Aquila: The Hospitable Teachers 73

Epaphroditus: The Devoted Worker......................................74

Chapter 14: Paul's Lesser-Known Fellow Workers............ 75

Asyncritus: The Unifying Worker..75

Hermas: The Faithful Servant 75

Julia: The Esteemed Sister..76

Philologus: The Knowledgeable Brother 76

Tychicus: The Faithful Messenger..76

Epaphras: The Dedicated Intercessor....................................77

Aristarchus: The Loyal Companion 77

Crescens: The Missionary to Galatia 78

Carpus: The Hospitable Host...78

Erastus: The City Treasurer..78

Theodotus: The Compassionate Caregiver 79

Chapter 15: Those Who Fell Away: Lessons from Alexander, Demas, Hermogenes, and Phygelus 80

Alexander: The Adversary of the Faith..................................80

Lessons from Alexander's Fall 80

Demas: The Lover of This World 81

Lessons from Demas's Fall..81

Hermogenes and Phygelus: The Deserters 82

Lessons from Hermogenes and Phygelus's Fall 82

Conclusion: Learning from Their Mistakes 83

Chapter 16: Paul's First Missionary Journey 84

The Commissioning at Antioch 84

Cyprus: Preaching in Salamis and Paphos 84

Perga and Pisidian Antioch 85

Iconium: Division and Perseverance 86

Lystra and Derbe: Miracles and Persecution 87

Returning to Strengthen the Churches 87

Reporting Back to Antioch 88

Chapter 17: Paul's Second Missionary Journey 89

The Disagreement and New Companions 89

Revisiting and Strengthening the Churches 89

Adding Timothy to the Team 90

The Macedonian Call 90

Philippi: The Conversion of Lydia and the Philippian Jailer .. 91

Thessalonica and Berea: Preaching and Opposition 91

Athens: Engaging the Philosophers 92

Corinth: A Prolonged Ministry 93

Return to Antioch 93

Chapter 18: Paul's Third Missionary Journey 95

Revisiting Galatia and Phrygia 95

The Extended Stay in Ephesus 95

Miracles and Opposition 96

Encouragement and Exhortation in Macedonia and Greece . 97

Return to Troas: Eutychus Revived 97

Farewell to the Ephesian Elders 98

Journey to Jerusalem: Prophecies and Warnings 98

Arrival in Jerusalem 99

Chapter 19: Paul's Arrest, First, and Second Imprisonments at Rome 100

Arrest in Jerusalem 100

Imprisonment in Caesarea 101

Journey to Rome 101

First Imprisonment in Rome 102

Release and Further Ministry 102

Second Imprisonment in Rome 103

Martyrdom and Legacy 103

Lessons from Paul's Imprisonments 104

Chapter 20: Paul: An Example Worthy of Imitation 105

Humility and Service 105

Perseverance in Suffering 106

Passion for the Gospel 106

Commitment to Discipleship 107

Love and Compassion 107

Faith and Hope 108

Paul's Call to Imitation 109

Conclusion: Paul's Enduring Legacy 109

Bibliography 110

Edward D. Andrews

Book Description

"The Teacher the Apostle Paul: What Made the Apostle Paul's Teaching, Preaching, Evangelism, and Apologetics Outstanding and Effective?" is an in-depth exploration of the remarkable teaching and evangelistic methods of the apostle Paul. This book delves into the unique aspects of Paul's approach that made his ministry profoundly impactful and enduring.

Starting with Paul's early education under Gamaliel, the book traces his background, conversion, and unique qualifications that equipped him for his mission. Readers will gain insights into Paul's theological contributions, his missionary journeys, and the strategies he employed to teach, preach, and defend the faith.

Each chapter offers a detailed analysis of Paul's methods, including his boldness in teaching, simplicity and clarity, use of questions, active listening, and respect for others. The book also addresses overcoming weaknesses in teaching, utilizing secular knowledge to defend the faith, and employing persuasion to lead others to Christ.

The book includes practical applications of Paul's strategies for modern Christians, emphasizing the importance of intellectual rigor, effective communication, and the integration of faith and reason. It highlights Paul's use of cultural contexts, philosophical reasoning, and historical knowledge to engage with diverse audiences.

Through examining Paul's relationships with fellow workers, such as Barnabas, Timothy, and Luke, and his mentorship of Timothy, the book showcases the importance of collaboration, mentorship, and mutual support in Christian ministry. It also explores the lessons learned from those who fell away from the faith and how believers can avoid similar pitfalls.

"The Teacher the Apostle Paul" provides a comprehensive look at Paul's vision of unity in the body of Christ, his theology of suffering and perseverance, and the enduring legacy of his teachings. This book is an invaluable resource for theologians, students of the Bible, and anyone seeking to understand the principles that made Paul's ministry so effective.

Join us in exploring the profound impact of Paul's teaching, preaching, evangelism, and apologetics, and discover how his example can inspire and guide Christians today.

Edward D. Andrews

Preface

The life and ministry of the apostle Paul stand as a testament to the transformative power of the Gospel and the profound impact one individual can have when fully committed to the service of Christ. Paul's journey from a persecutor of Christians to a foremost apostle and evangelist is a narrative rich with lessons on faith, perseverance, and dedication.

This book seeks to explore the various facets of Paul's teaching, preaching, evangelism, and apologetics that made his ministry exceptionally effective. It is not just an academic examination but also a practical guide for those who wish to understand and apply Paul's methods in their own ministry contexts.

The apostle Paul's approach was multifaceted, combining deep theological insight with practical strategies for teaching and evangelism. His ability to communicate complex truths with simplicity, his boldness in the face of opposition, and his unwavering commitment to the Gospel provide a model for effective ministry that is as relevant today as it was in the first century.

In preparing this book, I have aimed to present Paul's methods and strategies in a way that is both informative and applicable. Each chapter delves into specific aspects of his ministry, drawing from the Scriptures to provide a detailed understanding of how Paul taught, preached, and defended the faith. The goal is to equip readers with the knowledge and tools needed to enhance their own teaching and evangelistic efforts.

Throughout this book, we will explore the historical and cultural contexts of Paul's ministry, his interactions with various individuals and communities, and the enduring principles that can be gleaned from his example. Whether you are a pastor, a teacher, a student of the Bible, or a layperson seeking to deepen your understanding of Christian ministry, this book is designed to offer valuable insights and practical guidance.

As we journey through the pages of this book, may we be inspired by Paul's dedication, challenged by his example, and motivated to serve Christ with the same fervor and faithfulness. It is my hope that this exploration of Paul's ministry will not only enhance your knowledge but also ignite a passion for effective teaching, preaching, and evangelism in your own life.

Edward D. Andrews

Author of 220+ books

Edward D. Andrews

Introduction

The apostle Paul is a figure of immense significance in Christian history. His writings constitute a substantial portion of the New Testament, and his missionary journeys were pivotal in spreading Christianity throughout the Roman Empire. Yet, what truly sets Paul apart is not merely the breadth of his travels or the volume of his letters, but the profound effectiveness of his ministry. Understanding what made Paul's teaching, preaching, evangelism, and apologetics so outstanding and effective is essential for anyone seeking to follow in his footsteps.

This book embarks on a journey to uncover the principles and practices that underpinned Paul's ministry. By examining his life, methods, and teachings, we aim to extract timeless lessons that can be applied to contemporary Christian ministry. Paul's approach was dynamic, deeply rooted in Scripture, and remarkably adaptable to different cultural contexts. His ability to connect with diverse audiences, whether Jews, Greeks, or Romans, highlights his profound understanding of both the message of the Gospel and the people he sought to reach.

THE APOSTLE PAUL

One of the key aspects of Paul's effectiveness was his background and preparation. Trained under the esteemed rabbi Gamaliel, Paul possessed a thorough knowledge of Jewish law and tradition. His Roman citizenship and familiarity with Hellenistic culture further equipped him to bridge cultural divides and communicate the Gospel in a way that was both faithful to its Jewish roots and accessible to Gentile audiences.

Paul's conversion experience on the road to Damascus was another critical factor. This dramatic encounter with the risen Christ transformed him from a zealous persecutor of Christians into one of their most ardent advocates. The radical nature of his conversion added a powerful testimony to his message and provided a compelling example of the transformative power of the Gospel.

Throughout his ministry, Paul demonstrated a relentless commitment to his mission, often at great personal cost. He endured beatings, imprisonment, shipwrecks, and constant opposition. Yet, his perseverance in the face of such adversity serves as a powerful example of unwavering faith and dedication. Paul's letters, written during his imprisonments, reflect his deep theological insights and his pastoral concern for the churches he founded.

In addition to his personal qualities and experiences, Paul's methods of teaching and preaching were also highly effective. He employed a variety of techniques, including the use of questions, active listening, and persuasive reasoning. His ability to explain complex theological concepts with clarity and simplicity made his teachings accessible to all. Furthermore, Paul's use of cultural references and philosophical reasoning helped him engage with different audiences, making the Gospel relevant and compelling.

Paul's approach to evangelism was strategic and adaptable. He often began his ministry in a new city by preaching in the local synagogue, reaching out first to the Jewish community before turning to the Gentiles. His missionary journeys were meticulously planned, covering vast geographical areas and establishing strong, self-sustaining churches. Paul's letters to these churches provided ongoing guidance and support, ensuring that his influence extended far beyond his physical presence.

This book also explores Paul's use of apologetics in defending the faith. His ability to engage with different worldviews, address objections, and articulate the truth of the Gospel with intellectual rigor and spiritual authority is a testament to his deep understanding and commitment. Paul's encounters with philosophers in Athens, his defense before Roman authorities, and his correspondence with early Christian communities all highlight his skill in apologetics.

As we delve into the various aspects of Paul's ministry, our goal is not merely to admire his achievements but to learn from his example. By understanding what made Paul's teaching, preaching, evangelism, and apologetics so effective, we can better equip ourselves to carry out the Great Commission in our own contexts. Paul's life and ministry offer a blueprint for effective Christian witness, rooted in deep theological understanding, cultural awareness, and unwavering dedication to the Gospel.

Through this exploration, may we be inspired to emulate Paul's example, drawing from his wisdom and experience to enhance our own ministry efforts. As we study the apostle Paul, let us be reminded of the power of the Gospel and the transformative impact it can have on individuals and communities when faithfully proclaimed and lived out.

Chapter 1: Gamaliel Taught Saul of Tarsus

Many stood there calm and in still silence. Only a few moments earlier, they had attempted to kill the apostle Paul, also known by his Hebrew name, Saul of Tarsus. He had been saved by Roman troops and now faced the crowd of people from a stairway near the temple in Jerusalem.

Paul motioned the people with his hand to be silent and began to address them in Hebrew, saying:

"Brothers and fathers, hear the defense that I now make to you." And when they heard that he was addressing them in the Hebrew language, they became even more quiet. And he said, "I am a Jew, born in Tarsus in Cilicia, but brought up in this city, educated at the feet of Gamaliel according to the strict manner of the law of our fathers, being zealous for God as all of you are this day" (Acts 22:1-3, UASV).

Here stood Paul, his life hanging in the balance, and he begins his defense by saying that he was "educated at the feet of Gamaliel." Why? Who was this Gamaliel, and how could his being taught by him help Paul? Moreover, what all was involved in being taught by Gamaliel? What kind of impact did this training have on Saul, and did it influence him even after he became a Christian and an apostle?

Just Who Was Gamaliel?

Rabbi Gamaliel I, son of Simon and grandson (according to the Talmud) of Rabbi Hillel (founder of the more liberal of the two main schools of the Pharisees, Shammai being the other). Although an alternate tradition makes Gamaliel the son of Hillel, the Talmud is surely to be preferred on this point. A member of the Sanhedrin and a teacher of the law (Acts 5:34), he was known in rabbinical writings as Gamaliel the Elder to distinguish him from his grandson, Gamaliel II. He was the first of seven successive leaders of the school of Hillel to be honored with the title Rabban ("Our Rabbi/Master").

While believing the law of God to be divinely inspired, Gamaliel tended to emphasize its human elements. He recommended that Sabbath observance be less rigorous and burdensome, regulated current custom with respect to divorce in order to protect women, and urged kindness toward Gentiles. Scholarly, urbane, and a man of great intellect, he studied Greek literature avidly. His tolerance and cautious spirit are entirely in keeping with the account of his appeal in the Sanhedrin to spare the lives of Peter and his companions (Acts 5:33-39).

The Talmud mentions a student of Gamaliel who displayed "impudence in matters of learning," a young man identified by some as the apostle Paul. Paul himself says, "Under Gamaliel, I was thoroughly trained in the law of our fathers and was just as zealous for God as any of you are today" (Acts 22:3, UASV).

Several indications from elsewhere in the New Testament tend to corroborate Paul's claim as recorded by Luke. Although Paul usually quotes from the Septuagint when referring to Old Testament passages, he sometimes clearly makes use of the Hebrew text (Job 41:3 in Romans 11:35; Job 5:12 in 1 Corinthians 3:19; Exodus 16:18 in 2 Corinthians 8:15; Numbers 16:5 in 2 Timothy 2:19).

In Galatians 1:14, Paul mentions a period of advanced and specialized study of the very kind that one might expect under a teacher of Gamaliel's stature, and he does so in language strongly reminiscent of Acts 22:3: "I was advancing in Judaism beyond many Jews of my own age and was extremely zealous for the traditions of my fathers" (UASV).

In Philippians 3:6, Paul asserts that before his conversion to faith in Christ he was faultless as far as legalistic righteousness is concerned. Paul made use of five of the seven hermeneutical principles usually associated with Gamaliel's grandfather Hillel. This is understandable in the light of the fact that Gamaliel consistently and faithfully perpetuated the teachings and methodology of his grandfather. For example, Paul uses the hermeneutical principle of arguing from the lesser to the greater in 1 Corinthians 9:9-12, which begins as follows: "Do not muzzle an ox while it is treading out the grain." After thus quoting Deuteronomy 25:4, the apostle makes application—in typical

Halakic fashion—by stating that if God is concerned about oxen He is all the more concerned that His faithful human servants receive the support they deserve and need.

Luke's characteristic restraint in his references to Gamaliel in Acts may be contrasted with two later passages that also mention him. According to Clement Recognitions i.65, the apostle Peter states that Gamaliel was "our brother in the faith," and Photius asserts that he was baptized by Peter and Paul. But both of these traditions are now universally rejected as spurious. Gamaliel's reputation as one of the greatest teachers in the annals of Judaism, however, remains untarnished.

Jerusalem's temple was destroyed by the Roman army under General Titus in 70 C.E., killing one million one hundred thousand Jews and taking over one hundred thousand captives back to Rome. After the destruction, Bet Hillel (the House of Hillel) was preferred to Bet Shammai (the House of Shammai). The House of Hillel became the official form of Judaism, as all other parties died out with the destruction of the temple. The judgments, rulings, and decisions of Bet Hillel are often the basis for Jewish law in the Mishnah, which became the framework of the Talmud, and Gamaliel's influence was a significant factor in its dominant influence.

Gamaliel was so respected that he was the first to be called Rabban, a title higher than that of a Rabbi. In fact, "[Gamaliel] was so highly thought of that at his death it was said, 'When Rabban Gamaliel the elder died the glory of the Torah ceased and purity and saintliness perished' (Sot. 9:15, taken from Encyclopedia Judaica, vol. 7, p. 296)."

How Was Paul Taught by Gamaliel?

The apostle Paul told the crowd of people in Jerusalem that he was "educated at the feet of Gamaliel." What did Paul mean? Why was this important to his defense? What all was entailed in being a disciple of a teacher like Gamaliel?

The literal rendering says it all, "educated at the feet of Gamaliel," which is rendered by other translations as "educated under Gamaliel." The disciples (students) of such a rabbi as Gamaliel would literally sit at the feet of the teacher, taking in the scholar's words as one thirsting takes in water. The oral law would only remain accurate and reliable if there was this bond between the disciple and the teacher. The teacher would take great care in his teaching and the student would be extremely intent on learning it.

In his book "A History of the Jewish People in the Time of Jesus Christ," Emil Schürer sheds light on the methods of first-century rabbinic teachers. He writes: "The second chief task of the scribes was to teach the law. The ideal of legal Judaism was properly that every Israelite should have a professional acquaintance with the law. If this were unattainable, then the greatest possible number was to be raised to this ideal elevation. 'Bring up many scholars' is said to have been already a motto of the men of the Great Synagogue. Hence the more famous Rabbis often assembled about them in great numbers, youths desirous of instruction, for the purpose of making them thoroughly acquainted with the much ramified and copious 'oral law.' ... The instruction consisted of an indefatigable continuous exercise of the memory, For the object being that the pupils should remember with accuracy the entire matter with its thousands upon thousands of minutiae, and the oral law being never committed to writing, the instruction could not be confined to a single statement. The teacher was obliged to repeat his matter again and again with his pupils. Hence in Rabbinic diction 'to repeat' (שָׁנָה, δευτεροῦν) means exactly the same as 'to teach' (whence also מִשְׁנָה, teaching). This repetition was not, however, performed by the teacher only delivering his matter. The whole proceeding was, on the contrary, disputational. The teacher brought before his pupils several legal questions for their decision and let them answer them or answered them himself. The pupils were also allowed to propose questions to the teacher. This form of catechetical lecture has left its mark upon the style of the Mishna, the question being frequently started how this or that subject is to be understood for the purpose of giving a decision. All knowledge of the law being strictly traditional, a pupil had only two duties. One was to keep everything faithfully in memory. R. Dosthai said in the name of R. Meir: He who forgets a tenet of his instruction in the law, to him the Scripture imputes the willful forfeiture of his life. The second duty was never to teach anything otherwise than it had been delivered to him.

Even in expression he was to confine himself to the words of his teacher: 'Everyone is bound to teach with the expressions of his teacher.' It was the highest praise of a pupil to be 'like a well lined with lime, which loses not one drop.'"

Considering how the Rabbis taught, the risks for the pupils were far higher than just receiving a passing grade. The students who studied under such teachers were warned: "Whoever forgets a single thing from what he has learned—Scripture reckons it to him as if he has become liable for his life." The highest praise was bestowed upon a student who was like "a plastered well, which does not lose a drop of water." This was the type of training that Paul received when he was known by his Hebrew name Saul, as a young man, from Gamaliel.

The Teachings of Gamaliel

Gamaliel was a Pharisee of the highest order, so he promoted belief in the oral law. In this, he placed greater emphasis on the traditions of the rabbis than on inspired Scripture. (Mark 7:13; Matthew 15:3-9) The Mishnah quotes Gamaliel as saying: "Provide yourself with a teacher [a rabbi] and free yourself of doubt, for you must not give an excess tithe through guesswork." For the Jewish people, this meant that when the Hebrew Old Testament Scriptures did not clearly say what to do, they were not to interpret the Scriptures for themselves or follow their conscience to make a decision. Rather, they were to follow the interpretation of a qualified rabbi. It was Gamaliel's position that only in this way could an individual avoid sinning.

However, as was stated above, Gamaliel was generally well-known for his liberal attitude in his religious legal rulings. For example, he showed consideration for women when he ruled that he would "permit a wife to remarry on the testimony of a single witness [to her husband's death]." Furthermore, to defend a divorcée, Gamaliel presented several restrictions on the issue of a letter of divorce.

This liberal attitude is also seen in Gamaliel's dealings with the early disciples of Jesus Christ. In the book of Acts, we find other Jewish leaders who sought to kill Jesus' apostles after they had been arrested for preaching,

"But when they heard this, they were cut to the heart and were planning to kill them. But a Pharisee in the council named Gamaliel, a teacher of the law held in honor by all the people, stood up and gave orders to put the men outside for a little while. And he said to them, 'Men of Israel, take care what you are about to do with these men. For before these days Theudas rose up, claiming to be somebody, and a number of men, about four hundred, joined him. He was killed, and all who followed him were dispersed and came to nothing. After this man, Judas of Galilee rose up in the days of the census and drew away some people after him; he too perished, and all those who obeyed him were scattered. So in the present case, I tell you, stay away from these men and leave them alone, for if this plan or this work is of men, it will be overthrown; but if it is of God, you will not be able to overthrow them; or else you may even be found fighting against God.' At this, they were persuaded by him, and they summoned the apostles, flogged them, and ordered them not to speak in the name of Jesus, and let them go. So they went out from before the Sanhedrin, rejoicing that they were counted worthy to suffer dishonor for the name. And every day in the temple and from house to house they kept right on teaching and proclaiming the good news that the Christ was Jesus" (Acts 5:33-42, UASV).

What Did It Mean for Paul?

The apostle Paul had been trained and educated at the feet of one of the greatest rabbinic teachers of the first century C.E. Therefore, his mention of Gamaliel likely gave serious pause to the crowd in Jerusalem, moving them to pay special attention to his speech. Nevertheless, Paul told them of a far greater and more superior teacher than Gamaliel, Jesus Christ, the Messiah they had all been waiting for, who had already come. Paul now addressed these ones not as a disciple of Gamaliel but rather as a disciple of Jesus Christ.

"Brothers and fathers, hear the defense that I now make to you." And when they heard that he was addressing them in the Hebrew language, they became even more quiet. And he said, "I am a Jew, born in Tarsus in Cilicia, but brought up in this city, educated at the feet of

THE APOSTLE PAUL

Gamaliel according to the strict manner of the law of our fathers, being zealous for God as all of you are this day. I persecuted this Way to the death, binding and putting both men and women into prisons, as the high priest and the whole council of elders can testify about me. From them, I received letters to the brothers, and I journeyed toward Damascus in order to bring even those who were there in bonds to Jerusalem to be punished. And it happened that as I was traveling and approaching Damascus around noon, suddenly a very bright light from heaven flashed around me, and I fell to the ground and heard a voice saying to me, 'Saul, Saul, why are you persecuting me?' And I answered, 'Who are you, Lord?' And he said to me, 'I am Jesus of Nazareth, whom you are persecuting.' Now the men who were with me saw the light, indeed, but did not hear the voice of the one who was speaking to me. So I said, 'What should I do, Lord?' And the Lord said to me, 'Get up and go into Damascus, and there it will be told to you about all the things that have been appointed for you to do.' And since I could not see because of the brightness of that light, I was led by the hand by those who were with me and came into Damascus. And one Ananias, a devout man according to the law, well spoken of by all the Jews who lived there, came to me, and standing by me said to me, 'Brother Saul, receive your sight.' And at that very hour, I received my sight and saw him. And he said, 'The God of our fathers appointed you to know his will, to see the Righteous One and to hear a voice from his mouth; for you will be a witness for him to all men of what you have seen and heard. And now why do you wait? Rise and be baptized and wash away your sins, calling on his name.' It happened when I returned to Jerusalem and was praying in the temple, that I fell into a trance, and saw him saying to me, 'Make haste and get out of Jerusalem quickly, because they will not accept your testimony about me.' And I said, 'Lord, they themselves know that in one synagogue after another I imprisoned and beat those who believed in you. And when the blood of your witness Stephen was being shed, I myself also was standing near and was approving and was guarding the outer garments of those who were killing him.' And he said to me, 'Go, for I will send you far away to the Gentiles'" (Acts 22:1-21, UASV).

Was the apostle Paul influenced by Gamaliel when it came to his teaching as a Christian? Likely, the rigorous instruction in Scripture and Jewish law proved valuable to Paul as a Christian teacher. Yet, Paul's divinely inspired letters found in the Bible unquestionably show that he renounced the essence of the Pharisaic beliefs of Gamaliel. Paul led his fellow Jews and all others, not to the man-made traditions of the rabbis of Judaism, but to Jesus Christ.

If the apostle Paul had rejected Jesus Christ and remained a disciple of Gamaliel, he would have led a life of great privilege. Other students of Gamaliel helped to shape the future of Judaism.

For instance, Gamaliel's son Simeon ben Gamliel (I), possibly a fellow student of Paul, played a major role in the civil war, in the Jewish Revolt of 66-70 C.E. After the destruction of the temple, Rabban Gamaliel II "was the first person to lead the Sanhedrin as Nasi after the fall of the second temple. Gamaliel II was appointed Nasi approximately 10 years later." Gamaliel II's grandson Judah Ha-Nasi was the compiler of the Mishnah, which has become the basis of Jewish thought until our day.

As a student of Gamaliel, Saul of Tarsus might have become very powerful and prominent in Judaism. Yet, concerning such a career, Paul wrote: "But whatever things were gain to me, those things I have counted as loss for the sake of Christ. More than that, I count all things to be loss in view of the surpassing value of knowing Christ Jesus my Lord, for whom I have suffered the loss of all things, and count them but rubbish in order that I may gain Christ" (Philippians 3:7-8, UASV).

Paul was actually heeding the words of his teacher Gamaliel, who had said to guard against being "found fighters actually against God" by rejecting his pharisaical life and becoming a disciple of Jesus Christ. The moment Paul stopped persecuting the disciples of Jesus Christ, he stopped fighting against God. Rather, when he became a follower of Christ, he became one of "God's fellow workers" (1 Corinthians 3:9).

Today, true zealous Christians are to proclaim the same message. Just as was true of Paul, many today have had to make dramatic changes in their lives. Some have even given up a life of privilege. They have followed the example of Paul, as opposed to his former teacher, Gamaliel.

Chapter 2: Why Paul?

Paul, also known as Saul of Tarsus, is one of the most influential figures in the history of Christianity. His life and works have had a profound impact on the development of Christian theology and the spread of the Gospel. Understanding why Paul was chosen and how his background uniquely prepared him for his mission is crucial for appreciating his contributions.

Paul's Background and Conversion

Saul of Tarsus was born in Tarsus, a major city in Cilicia, known for its education and culture. He was a Roman citizen by birth, which afforded him certain privileges and protections. However, his early life was marked by his fervent adherence to Judaism. Saul was a Pharisee, educated under the renowned Rabbi Gamaliel, which provided him with a deep understanding of the Hebrew Scriptures and Jewish traditions.

Saul's zealousness for the Jewish faith led him to persecute early Christians, whom he viewed as a threat to Judaism. He was present at the stoning of Stephen, the first Christian martyr, and he actively sought to imprison Christians. However, on his way to Damascus to arrest more Christians, Saul had a life-changing encounter with Jesus Christ. As he later recounted:

"Now as he went on his way, he approached Damascus, and suddenly a light from heaven shone around him. And falling to the ground, he heard a voice saying to him, 'Saul, Saul, why are you persecuting me?' And he said, 'Who are you, Lord?' And he said, 'I am Jesus, whom you are persecuting. But rise and enter the city, and you will be told what you are to do.'" (Acts 9:3-6, UASV)

This encounter marked the beginning of Saul's transformation into Paul, the apostle of Jesus Christ. After being blinded and led into Damascus, a disciple named Ananias, directed by the Lord, restored Saul's sight and baptized him. Saul immediately began preaching that

Jesus is the Son of God, astonishing those who knew him as a fierce opponent of Christianity.

The Unique Qualifications of Paul

Paul's background uniquely qualified him for his mission as the apostle to the Gentiles. His education under Gamaliel provided him with a thorough knowledge of the Scriptures, which he skillfully used to argue that Jesus was the promised Messiah. His Roman citizenship allowed him to travel freely across the Roman Empire, and his familiarity with Greek culture and language enabled him to communicate effectively with Gentiles.

Paul's fervor and zeal, once directed towards persecuting Christians, were now redirected towards spreading the Gospel. His writings and missionary journeys played a crucial role in establishing Christian communities and addressing theological issues within the early Church.

Paul's Theological Contributions

Paul's letters, which form a significant portion of the New Testament, address a wide range of theological topics. His writings emphasize salvation by grace through faith, the role of Jesus Christ as the fulfillment of the law, and the importance of unity within the body of Christ. Some key passages include:

"For by grace you have been saved through faith; and that not of yourselves, it is the gift of God; not as a result of works, so that no one may boast." (Ephesians 2:8-9, UASV)

"Christ is the end of the law for righteousness to everyone who believes." (Romans 10:4, UASV)

"There is neither Jew nor Greek, there is neither slave nor free man, there is neither male nor female; for you are all one in Christ Jesus." (Galatians 3:28, UASV)

Paul's teachings on justification, sanctification, and the nature of the Church have had a lasting impact on Christian doctrine. His letters address practical issues facing early Christian communities and provide guidance on living a life that honors God.

Paul's Missionary Journeys

Paul undertook several missionary journeys to spread the Gospel. His travels took him throughout the Roman Empire, including Asia Minor, Greece, and Rome. He faced numerous hardships, including imprisonment, beatings, and shipwrecks, but remained steadfast in his mission.

One of the most significant events during his missionary work was the Council of Jerusalem, where Paul argued that Gentile converts should not be required to follow the Mosaic Law. The council's decision to exempt Gentiles from circumcision and dietary laws was a pivotal moment in the history of the early Church, helping to define the nature of Christian identity.

Paul's strategy often involved first preaching in synagogues to Jews and then turning to the Gentiles. This approach is evident in his visit to Antioch of Pisidia, where he declared:

"It was necessary that the word of God should be spoken first to you. Since you thrust it aside and judge yourselves unworthy of eternal life, behold, we are turning to the Gentiles. For so the Lord has commanded us, saying, 'I have made you a light for the Gentiles, that you may bring salvation to the ends of the earth.'" (Acts 13:46-47, UASV)

The Enduring Legacy of Paul

Paul's influence extends beyond his writings and missionary journeys. His life exemplifies the transformative power of the Gospel and the importance of obedience to God's call. Despite his past as a persecutor of Christians, Paul became one of the most dedicated and effective apostles, demonstrating that God's grace can redeem and use anyone for His purposes.

Paul's example challenges Christians to be bold in their faith, to engage thoughtfully with both Scripture and culture, and to be unwavering in their commitment to spreading the Gospel. His letters continue to be a source of inspiration and guidance for believers, providing timeless truths that are as relevant today as they were in the first century.

In conclusion, Paul's life and ministry were marked by his profound encounter with Christ, his unique qualifications and background, and his unwavering commitment to spreading the Gospel. His contributions to Christian theology and the early Church have had a lasting impact, making him one of the most significant figures in the history of Christianity.

Chapter 3: Why You?

Paul, the apostle, faced unique challenges and opportunities in his mission to spread the Gospel. His background, education, and personal experiences played significant roles in shaping his approach to evangelism and apologetics.

Paul's Conversion and Early Life

Saul of Tarsus, as Paul was known before his conversion, was a fervent Pharisee, deeply committed to Judaism. Born in Tarsus, a major city in Cilicia, he was also a Roman citizen, which afforded him certain privileges and protections. His education under Gamaliel, a respected teacher of the law, provided him with an extensive knowledge of the Hebrew Scriptures and Jewish traditions. This background was crucial for his later work as an apostle.

Paul's transformation from a persecutor of Christians to a dedicated apostle began on the road to Damascus. As he was traveling to arrest Christians, he encountered Jesus Christ in a dramatic vision. This event is described in Acts 9:3-6 (UASV):

"Now as he went on his way, he approached Damascus, and suddenly a light from heaven shone around him. And falling to the ground, he heard a voice saying to him, 'Saul, Saul, why are you persecuting me?' And he said, 'Who are you, Lord?' And he said, 'I am Jesus, whom you are persecuting. But rise and enter the city, and you will be told what you are to do.'"

Blinded by the vision, Saul was led into Damascus, where a disciple named Ananias restored his sight and baptized him. This marked the beginning of Saul's transformation into Paul, the apostle.

Unique Qualifications for Apostleship

Paul's unique background equipped him for his mission to the Gentiles. His education under Gamaliel provided him with a thorough understanding of the Scriptures, which he used to argue that Jesus was the promised Messiah. His Roman citizenship allowed him to travel freely across the Roman Empire, and his familiarity with Greek culture and language enabled him to communicate effectively with Gentiles.

Paul's zeal, once directed towards persecuting Christians, was now channeled into spreading the Gospel. His missionary journeys took him to various parts of the Roman Empire, including Asia Minor, Greece, and Rome. He faced numerous hardships, including imprisonment, beatings, and shipwrecks, but remained steadfast in his mission.

Theological Contributions

Paul's letters, which form a significant portion of the New Testament, address a wide range of theological topics. His writings emphasize salvation by grace through faith, the role of Jesus Christ as the fulfillment of the law, and the importance of unity within the body of Christ. Key passages include:

"For by grace you have been saved through faith; and that not of yourselves, it is the gift of God; not as a result of works, so that no one may boast." (Ephesians 2:8-9, UASV)

"Christ is the end of the law for righteousness to everyone who believes." (Romans 10:4, UASV)

"There is neither Jew nor Greek, there is neither slave nor free man, there is neither male nor female; for you are all one in Christ Jesus." (Galatians 3:28, UASV)

Paul's teachings on justification, sanctification, and the nature of the Church have had a lasting impact on Christian doctrine. His letters address practical issues facing early Christian communities and provide guidance on living a life that honors God.

Evangelistic Strategies

Paul's approach to evangelism involved both direct preaching and reasoned argumentation. He often began his ministry in a new city by preaching in the local synagogue to Jews before turning to the Gentiles.

This strategy is evident in his visit to Antioch of Pisidia, where he declared:

"It was necessary that the word of God should be spoken first to you. Since you thrust it aside and judge yourselves unworthy of eternal life, behold, we are turning to the Gentiles. For so the Lord has commanded us, saying, 'I have made you a light for the Gentiles, that you may bring salvation to the ends of the earth.'" (Acts 13:46-47, UASV)

Paul's ability to adapt his message to different audiences was a key factor in his success. He used his knowledge of the Scriptures to reason with Jews and employed philosophical arguments when addressing Gentiles. His speech at the Areopagus in Athens (Acts 17:22-31) is a prime example of his skill in engaging with a diverse audience.

Paul's Endurance and Commitment

Despite the numerous challenges he faced, Paul remained committed to his mission. He endured imprisonment, beatings, and other hardships for the sake of the Gospel. His letters reveal a deep love for the churches he founded and a strong desire to see believers grow in their faith. In his letter to the Philippians, he wrote:

"But whatever things were gain to me, those things I have counted as loss for the sake of Christ. More than that, I count all things to be loss in view of the surpassing value of knowing Christ Jesus my Lord, for whom I have suffered the loss of all things, and count them but rubbish in order that I may gain Christ." (Philippians 3:7-8, UASV)

Paul's endurance and commitment serve as an example for Christians today. His life demonstrates the transformative power of the Gospel and the importance of obedience to God's call. His teachings continue to inspire and guide believers in their walk with Christ.

In conclusion, Paul's unique background, profound conversion experience, and unwavering commitment to spreading the Gospel make him a pivotal figure in the history of Christianity. His contributions to Christian theology and his example of faithfulness and perseverance continue to impact believers worldwide.

Chapter 4: Paul's Effective Strategies of Teaching

The writings of Luke and Paul include numerous examples of effective teaching strategies employed by Paul. These examples illustrate Paul's practical application of various teaching methods, which can be applied to evangelism and apologetics today.

Paul's Methods of Teaching

Paul's effectiveness as a teacher stemmed from his ability to adapt his methods to the needs of his audience. His strategies included collaborative teaching, mentoring, and the use of boldness, simplicity, and questions in his approach. This section delves into these methods and provides insights on how they can be used in modern evangelism.

Teaching, Preaching, Evangelism, and Apologetics

Paul's teaching methods can be categorized into four main areas: teaching, preaching, evangelism, and apologetics. Each area serves a distinct purpose but often overlaps in practice. Teaching involves imparting new knowledge and demonstrating skills. Preaching shares messages of faith, spreading the gospel, and encouraging Christian behavior. Evangelism focuses on converting others to Christianity, while apologetics defends the faith through sound reasoning and evidence.

Examples of Paul's Boldness in Teaching

Paul's boldness is evident throughout his missionary journeys. In Acts 18:4, it is recorded that Paul "reasoned in the synagogue every Sabbath, trying to persuade Jews and Greeks." His willingness to engage in public debate and confront opposition head-on is a testament to his confidence in the truth of the gospel. This boldness was not arrogance but a deep conviction born out of his personal encounter with Christ and his thorough understanding of Scripture.

Simplicity and Clarity in Teaching

Paul often used simplicity in his teaching to ensure his message was clear and accessible. For instance, in 1 Corinthians 2:1-2, he states, "And when I came to you, brothers, I did not come proclaiming to you the testimony of God with lofty speech or wisdom. For I decided to know nothing among you except Jesus Christ and him crucified." By focusing on the core message of the gospel, Paul avoided unnecessary complexity and made the truth clear to all.

Use of Questions in Teaching

Paul's use of questions was a powerful tool in his teaching strategy. He often employed questions to provoke thought and engage his audience in deeper reflection. For example, in Romans 3:1, he asks, "Then what advantage has the Jew? Or what is the value of circumcision?" These questions not only challenged his listeners to think critically but also provided a framework for his subsequent teachings.

Active Listening and Respect for Others

Paul's interactions with others demonstrate his respect and active listening skills. In Acts 17:22-23, when addressing the Athenians at the Areopagus, he begins by acknowledging their religious fervor and then uses their altar to an unknown god as a starting point for his message about Jehovah. This approach shows Paul's sensitivity to his audience's beliefs and his ability to connect with them on common ground.

Irrefutable Logic and Use of Scripture

Paul's teaching was characterized by his logical reasoning and thorough use of Scripture. In Acts 17:2-3, it is noted that "Paul went in, as was his custom, and on three Sabbath days he reasoned with them from the Scriptures, explaining and proving that it was necessary for the Christ to suffer and to rise from the dead, and saying, 'This Jesus, whom I proclaim to you, is the Christ.'" By grounding his arguments in Scripture, Paul provided a solid foundation for his teachings and made a compelling case for the truth of the gospel.

Hyperbole in Teaching

Paul also used hyperbole to emphasize his points. For example, in Galatians 1:8, he states, "But even if we or an angel from heaven should preach to you a gospel contrary to the one we preached to you, let him be accursed." This strong language underscores the importance of adhering to the true gospel and highlights the severity of deviating from it.

Collaborative Teaching and Mentoring

Paul's collaborative approach to teaching is evident in his relationships with fellow workers like Barnabas and Timothy. By working together, they were able to support and learn from each other, enhancing their ministry's effectiveness. Paul's mentoring of Timothy, in particular, shows his commitment to raising up new leaders and ensuring the continuity of the gospel message. In 2 Timothy 2:2, Paul instructs Timothy, "and what you have heard from me in the presence of many witnesses entrust to faithful men who will be able to teach others also."

Applying Paul's Strategies Today

The teaching strategies used by Paul can be applied effectively in contemporary evangelism and apologetics. By incorporating boldness, simplicity, questions, active listening, logical reasoning, and collaborative efforts, modern-day Christians can communicate the gospel message clearly and persuasively. Understanding Paul's methods and adapting them to current contexts will help in effectively spreading the faith and defending it against opposition.

Chapter 5: Teach with Insight and Persuasiveness

In the context of Christian teaching and evangelism, effective communication is vital for conveying the truths of the Gospel and for nurturing the faith of new believers. The apostle Paul serves as an exemplary model in this regard, demonstrating various methods and strategies that are both insightful and persuasive.

The Importance of Being a Good Listener

One of Paul's most notable skills was his ability to listen actively and attentively to those he taught. This skill is crucial for understanding the needs and concerns of others, allowing a teacher to address them effectively. Active listening involves more than just hearing words; it requires engaging with the speaker, understanding their perspective, and responding thoughtfully.

For instance, in Acts 17:22-23, Paul addresses the people of Athens by acknowledging their religious devotion: "Men of Athens, I perceive that in every way you are very religious. For as I passed along and observed the objects of your worship, I found also an altar with this inscription, 'To the unknown god.' What therefore you worship as unknown, this I proclaim to you" (UASV). By starting with their existing beliefs, Paul demonstrates respect and understanding, creating a bridge for his message about Jesus Christ.

Using Questions to Dig Deeper

Paul frequently used questions as a tool to provoke thought and encourage deeper engagement with his teachings. Questions can help clarify understanding, reveal underlying beliefs, and stimulate reflection. In Acts 19:2, Paul asks the disciples in Ephesus, "Did you receive the Holy Spirit when you believed?" This question not only clarifies their spiritual experience but also sets the stage for further instruction about the Holy Spirit and the fullness of Christian faith.

Understanding How Unbelievers Hear Christians

Recognizing how unbelievers perceive Christian messages is essential for effective communication. Many may have preconceived notions or misunderstandings about Christianity. Paul's approach in addressing these misunderstandings was to use language and concepts familiar to his audience, thereby reducing resistance and opening hearts to the truth. For example, in 1 Corinthians 9:19-22, Paul explains his method: "For though I am free from all, I have made myself a servant to all, that I might win more of them... I have become all things to all people, that by all means I might save some" (UASV). This flexibility and empathy in communication helped Paul connect with a diverse range of people.

Effective Listening and Responding

Effective teaching involves not just speaking but also listening and responding appropriately. Paul exemplified this by tailoring his responses to the specific needs and questions of his audience. In Acts 17:32-34, after Paul speaks about the resurrection, some mocked while others were curious. Paul responds by continuing to engage with those who were open, leading some to believe. This shows the importance of discerning and focusing efforts where there is receptivity.

Speaking with Purpose

Paul's teachings were characterized by clarity and purpose. He focused on delivering the core message of the Gospel without unnecessary complexity. This can be seen in his letter to the Corinthians: "For I decided to know nothing among you except Jesus Christ and him crucified" (1 Corinthians 2:2, UASV). By emphasizing the central tenet of Christian faith, Paul ensured that his message was clear and impactful.

The Value of Simplicity

Simplicity in teaching helps in making the message understandable and relatable. Paul often employed straightforward language and relatable examples to convey profound truths. His use of everyday metaphors and analogies helped make complex theological concepts accessible. For instance, in 2 Timothy 2:3-6, Paul uses the images of a soldier, an athlete, and a farmer to illustrate the discipline and dedication required in the Christian life.

Effective Use of Questions

Questions were a significant part of Paul's teaching toolkit, not just for clarification but also for engaging his audience in deeper thought. In Romans 3:1-2, Paul asks, "Then what advantage has the Jew? Or what is the value of circumcision?" These questions lead to a discussion on the faithfulness of God and the role of the Jewish people, prompting his readers to think critically about their own beliefs and assumptions.

Explaining and Proving

Paul's ability to explain and prove the truths of the Gospel was central to his teaching. He used logical arguments and scriptural evidence to support his claims, ensuring that his teachings were not just persuasive but also grounded in the authority of Scripture. In Acts 17:2-3, it is noted that Paul "reasoned with them from the Scriptures, explaining and proving that it was necessary for the Christ to suffer and to rise from the dead, and saying, 'This Jesus, whom I proclaim to you, is the Christ'" (UASV). This method of reasoning from the Scriptures provided a strong foundation for his teachings and helped convince many of the truth of the Gospel.

By adopting these strategies—listening actively, using questions effectively, understanding the audience, speaking with purpose, and grounding teachings in scriptural evidence—modern Christians can enhance their own teaching and evangelism efforts. Paul's example offers valuable insights into how to communicate the Gospel message in a way that is both persuasive and deeply impactful.

Edward D. Andrews

Chapter 6: Overcoming the Weaknesses in Our Teaching

Understanding and addressing the weaknesses in our teaching is crucial for effective ministry. Paul's methods and strategies provide us with a solid foundation for improving our own approach to teaching and evangelizing.

Recognizing Weaknesses

The first step in overcoming weaknesses is recognizing them. Often, these weaknesses stem from a lack of preparation, a failure to understand the audience, or ineffective communication methods. Paul's letters offer insights into how to address these issues.

Preparation and Study

Preparation is fundamental to effective teaching. Paul emphasized the importance of study and preparation in his letters to Timothy. In 2 Timothy 2:15, he urges, "Do your best to present yourself to God as one approved, a workman who does not need to be ashamed, rightly handling the word of truth" (UASV). This involves not only understanding the Scriptures but also being able to explain and apply them effectively.

Understanding the Audience

Paul's approach varied depending on his audience. In Athens, he addressed the philosophers by referencing their own poets and beliefs (Acts 17:28). In his letters to the Corinthians, he adapted his message to address their specific issues and misunderstandings. By understanding his audience, Paul could tailor his message to be more relevant and compelling.

Effective Communication

Communication is at the heart of teaching. Paul's letters are filled with examples of clear, concise, and compelling communication. He often used rhetorical questions to engage his audience and provoke thought. For example, in Romans 6:1-2, he asks, "What shall we say then? Are we to continue in sin that grace may abound? By no means!" (UASV). This method not only captures attention but also encourages deeper reflection.

Addressing Misunderstandings

Paul was adept at addressing misunderstandings and correcting errors. In his letter to the Galatians, he confronts the false teachings that had infiltrated the church. He writes, "I am astonished that you are so quickly deserting him who called you in the grace of Christ and are turning to a different gospel—not that there is another one, but there are some who trouble you and want to distort the gospel of Christ" (Galatians 1:6-7, UASV). By directly addressing the issue, Paul provides clarity and reaffirms the true gospel.

Utilizing Questions

Questions are a powerful tool in teaching. They encourage engagement and critical thinking. Paul used questions extensively to challenge his readers and lead them to deeper understanding. In 1 Corinthians 1:13, he asks, "Is Christ divided? Was Paul crucified for you? Or were you baptized in the name of Paul?" (UASV). These questions highlight the absurdity of divisions within the church and refocus the believers on Christ.

Simplifying Complex Concepts

One of Paul's strengths was his ability to simplify complex theological concepts. In his letter to the Romans, he explains justification by faith using the example of Abraham. He writes, "For what does the Scripture say? 'Abraham believed God, and it was counted to him as righteousness'" (Romans 4:3, UASV). By using familiar examples, Paul makes complex doctrines accessible and understandable.

Engaging Through Narrative

Paul often used narrative to make his points more relatable. His recounting of his own conversion experience in Acts 22 serves as a powerful testimony to the transformative power of the gospel. By sharing personal stories, Paul connects with his audience on a deeper level, making his message more impactful.

Encouragement and Exhortation

Paul's letters are filled with encouragement and exhortation. He knew that building up the church required more than just correction; it also required uplifting and motivating the believers. In 1 Thessalonians 5:11, he writes, "Therefore encourage one another and build one another up, just as you are doing" (UASV). This positive reinforcement helps to foster a supportive and loving community.

Being Adaptive and Flexible

Paul's adaptability was key to his effectiveness. He was willing to change his approach based on the situation and the needs of his audience. In 1 Corinthians 9:22, he states, "I have become all things to all people, that by all means I might save some" (UASV). This flexibility allowed him to reach a diverse range of people and address a variety of issues effectively.

Practical Application

Teaching should always aim for practical application. Paul consistently linked doctrine with daily living, providing practical advice on how to live out the faith. In Ephesians 4:1-3, he writes, "I therefore, a prisoner for the Lord, urge you to walk in a manner worthy of the calling to which you have been called, with all humility and gentleness, with patience, bearing with one another in love, eager to maintain the unity of the Spirit in the bond of peace" (UASV). By connecting theological truths with practical actions, Paul helps believers apply their faith in everyday life.

Building Confidence in the Message

Confidence in the message is essential for effective teaching. Paul's conviction and certainty are evident throughout his letters. In 2 Timothy 1:12, he declares, "But I am not ashamed, for I know whom I have believed, and I am convinced that he is able to guard until that Day what has been entrusted to me" (UASV). This confidence inspires trust and credibility, encouraging others to believe and follow the message.

By adopting these strategies and continuously striving to improve, we can overcome weaknesses in our teaching and become more effective in sharing the gospel and nurturing the faith of others.

Edward D. Andrews

Chapter 7: Paul's Use of Secular Knowledge to Defend the Faith

The apostle Paul masterfully utilized his understanding of secular knowledge to defend and spread the Christian faith. His ability to integrate cultural and philosophical references into his teaching and evangelism efforts allowed him to connect with diverse audiences and effectively communicate the truths of the Gospel. This chapter explores how Paul employed secular knowledge in his ministry and provides insights into how modern Christians can follow his example.

Engaging with Cultural Contexts

Paul's familiarity with various cultural contexts enabled him to communicate effectively with different groups. For instance, in Acts 17:22-23, Paul addresses the Athenians at the Areopagus by acknowledging their religious practices: "Men of Athens, I perceive that in every way you are very religious. For as I passed along and observed the objects of your worship, I found also an altar with this inscription, 'To the unknown god.' What therefore you worship as unknown, this I proclaim to you" (UASV). By referencing their altar, Paul bridges the gap between their beliefs and the truth of the Gospel, making his message more accessible.

Utilizing Philosophical Reasoning

Paul's background in Jewish and Greek education allowed him to use philosophical reasoning to defend the faith. In his letters, Paul often employed logical arguments and rhetorical techniques common in Greek philosophy. For example, in 1 Corinthians 15:12-19, Paul uses logical reasoning to argue for the resurrection of Christ: "But if there is no resurrection of the dead, then not even Christ has been raised. And if Christ has not been raised, then our preaching is in vain and your faith is in vain" (UASV). This method of reasoning would have resonated with those familiar with philosophical discourse.

Addressing Different Worldviews

Paul was adept at addressing various worldviews, whether he was speaking to Jews, Gentiles, or philosophers. In 1 Corinthians 9:19-22, Paul explains his approach: "For though I am free from all, I have made myself a servant to all, that I might win more of them... I have become all things to all people, that by all means I might save some" (UASV). This flexibility allowed Paul to present the Gospel in a way that was relevant and compelling to different audiences.

Quoting Secular Sources

Paul occasionally quoted secular sources to support his arguments. In Acts 17:28, he cites a Greek poet: "for 'In him we live and move and have our being'; as even some of your own poets have said, 'For we are indeed his offspring'" (UASV). By using familiar references, Paul demonstrated his knowledge of their literature and philosophy, which helped establish common ground and build credibility with his audience.

Integrating Historical Context

Understanding the historical context of Paul's ministry is crucial for appreciating his use of secular knowledge. Paul's Roman citizenship and education in Tarsus, a center of learning, provided him with a broad perspective. His ability to navigate different cultural settings and engage with various intellectual traditions was instrumental in his evangelistic efforts.

Practical Application for Modern Christians

Modern Christians can learn from Paul's example by integrating cultural and intellectual understanding into their own evangelism and apologetics. This involves being well-versed in the cultural and philosophical backgrounds of the people they are trying to reach. Christians should strive to understand the beliefs and values of their audience, using this knowledge to present the Gospel in a relevant and compelling manner.

Christians should also be prepared to engage with contemporary philosophical and cultural issues. This means staying informed about current events, popular beliefs, and philosophical trends. By doing so, they can address the concerns and questions of modern audiences effectively.

Developing Intellectual Rigor

Paul's example highlights the importance of intellectual rigor in defending the faith. Christians should cultivate a deep understanding of both Scripture and secular knowledge, integrating these insights to present a well-rounded and persuasive case for the Gospel. This requires diligent study, critical thinking, and the ability to communicate complex ideas clearly and effectively.

Balancing Faith and Reason

Paul's ministry demonstrates the harmony between faith and reason. He used logical arguments and philosophical reasoning to support the truths of the Gospel, showing that faith is not contrary to reason but is supported by it. Christians today should strive to balance faith and reason in their own witness, using rational arguments to support their faith while also relying on the transformative power of the Holy Spirit.

Emphasizing the Power of the Gospel

While Paul utilized secular knowledge and intellectual arguments, he always emphasized the power of the Gospel itself. In 1 Corinthians 2:1-5, Paul writes, "And I, when I came to you, brothers, did not come proclaiming to you the testimony of God with lofty speech or wisdom. For I decided to know nothing among you except Jesus Christ and him crucified... that your faith might not rest in the wisdom of men but in the power of God" (UASV). Ultimately, it is the message of Christ that transforms lives, and this should remain the focus of all evangelistic efforts.

By learning from Paul's example and integrating secular knowledge with a firm commitment to the Gospel, modern Christians can effectively communicate the truths of their faith in a way that resonates with diverse audiences. This approach not only honors the intellectual heritage of Christianity but also demonstrates the relevance and power of the Gospel in today's world.

Edward D. Andrews

Chapter 8: Use Persuasion to Help Others to Accept Jesus Christ & Defend Your Faith

The art of persuasion is critical in Christian evangelism and apologetics. Paul's defense before Agrippa, as documented in Acts, provides a remarkable example of persuasive evangelism. This chapter explores Paul's approach to persuasion, examining how he skillfully communicated the Gospel and defended his faith.

Paul Before Agrippa and Bernice

In 58 C.E., King Agrippa and his sister Bernice visited Caesarea to welcome the new governor, Festus. After several days, Festus discussed Paul's case with Agrippa. Paul had been arrested in Jerusalem and was facing accusations from the Jewish leaders. Festus sought Agrippa's advice on how to handle Paul's appeal to Caesar.

Acts 25:13-23 (UASV) provides the background: "Now when some days had passed, Agrippa the king and Bernice arrived at Caesarea and greeted Festus. And while they were staying there many days, Festus laid Paul's case before the king, saying, 'There is a man left prisoner by Felix, and when I was at Jerusalem, the chief priests and the elders of the Jews laid out their case against him, asking for a sentence of condemnation against him.'"

Paul's Defense Before Agrippa

Paul's defense before Agrippa is one of the most detailed accounts of his trial. Paul seized the opportunity to present his case and share his testimony. His approach was both respectful and assertive, using his knowledge of Jewish customs and Roman law to his advantage.

Acts 26:1-3 (UASV): "So Agrippa said to Paul, 'You have permission to speak for yourself.' Then Paul stretched out his hand and made his defense: 'I consider myself fortunate that it is before you,

King Agrippa, I am going to make my defense today against all the accusations of the Jews, especially because you are familiar with all the customs and controversies of the Jews. Therefore, I beg you to listen to me patiently.'"

Paul's Explanation of His Conversion

Paul recounted his conversion experience on the road to Damascus. He described how he had been a zealous persecutor of Christians until he encountered Jesus Christ. This personal testimony was powerful, demonstrating the transformative power of the Gospel.

Acts 26:12-18 (UASV): "In this connection I journeyed to Damascus with the authority and commission of the chief priests. At midday, O king, I saw on the way a light from heaven, brighter than the sun, that shone around me and those who journeyed with me. And when we had all fallen to the ground, I heard a voice saying to me in the Hebrew language, 'Saul, Saul, why are you persecuting me? It is hard for you to kick against the goads.' And I said, 'Who are you, Lord?' And the Lord said, 'I am Jesus whom you are persecuting. But rise and stand upon your feet, for I have appeared to you for this purpose, to appoint you as a servant and witness to the things in which you have seen me and to those in which I will appear to you, delivering you from your people and from the Gentiles—to whom I am sending you to open their eyes, so that they may turn from darkness to light and from the power of Satan to God, that they may receive forgiveness of sins and a place among those who are sanctified by faith in me.'"

Festus' and Agrippa's Responses

After Paul's defense, Festus and Agrippa had different reactions. Festus, a Roman governor unfamiliar with Jewish beliefs, thought Paul was mad. Agrippa, however, was more familiar with Jewish customs and Scripture. He acknowledged the persuasiveness of Paul's arguments.

Acts 26:24-28 (UASV): "And as he was saying these things in his defense, Festus said with a loud voice, 'Paul, you are out of your mind; your great learning is driving you out of your mind.' But Paul said, 'I am not out of my mind, most excellent Festus, but I am speaking true and rational words. For the king knows about these things, and to him I speak boldly. For I am persuaded that none of these things has escaped his notice, for this has not been done in a corner. King Agrippa, do you believe the prophets? I know that you believe.' And Agrippa said to Paul, 'In a short time would you persuade me to be a Christian?'"

Using the Art of Persuasion

Paul's use of persuasion was masterful. He combined logical reasoning, personal testimony, and Scriptural references to make a compelling case for the Gospel. His approach offers valuable lessons for modern Christian apologists and evangelists.

To persuade effectively, it is essential to understand the audience and address their beliefs and concerns respectfully. Paul's knowledge of Jewish customs and Roman law allowed him to connect with both Jewish and Gentile audiences. Similarly, modern evangelists should strive to understand the cultural and intellectual backgrounds of those they seek to reach.

Persuasion That Appeals to the Heart

Paul's testimony was not just a logical argument but an appeal to the heart. By sharing his personal experience, he demonstrated the transformative power of the Gospel. This approach helps to build trust and makes the message more relatable.

Acts 26:9-11 (UASV): "I myself was convinced that I ought to do many things in opposing the name of Jesus of Nazareth. And I did so in Jerusalem. I not only locked up many of the saints in prison after receiving authority from the chief priests, but when they were put to death I cast my vote against them. And I punished them often in all the synagogues and tried to make them blaspheme, and in raging fury against them I persecuted them even to foreign cities."

Using the Word of God Skillfully

Paul's arguments were firmly rooted in Scripture. He used the Word of God to validate his points and show that his message was consistent with the Jewish Scriptures. This approach not only provided authority to his message but also demonstrated his respect for the audience's beliefs.

Acts 26:22-23 (UASV): "To this day I have had the help that comes from God, and so I stand here testifying both to small and great, saying nothing but what the prophets and Moses said would come to pass: that the Christ must suffer and that, by being the first to rise from the dead, he would proclaim light both to our people and to the Gentiles."

Have God's View of Christian Apologetic Evangelism

Paul's example shows the importance of having a God-centered view of evangelism. His ultimate goal was not just to win arguments but to bring people to a saving knowledge of Jesus Christ. Modern evangelists should keep this focus, using persuasion not as a tool for personal victory but as a means to glorify God and draw others to Him.

1 Corinthians 2:1-5 (UASV): "And I, when I came to you, brothers, did not come proclaiming to you the testimony of God with lofty speech or wisdom. For I decided to know nothing among you except Jesus Christ and him crucified. And I was with you in weakness and in fear and much trembling, and my speech and my message were not in plausible words of wisdom, but in demonstration of the Spirit and of power, so that your faith might not rest in the wisdom of men but in the power of God."

How to Be Successful in Sharing God's Word

To be successful in sharing God's Word, Christians must combine knowledge of Scripture with effective communication skills. This involves being well-prepared, understanding the audience, using logical reasoning, and appealing to the heart. It also requires a deep personal conviction and reliance on the Holy Spirit for guidance and strength.

By following Paul's example and employing these strategies, modern Christians can effectively use persuasion to help others accept Jesus Christ and defend their faith.

Chapter 9: Paul's Letter to Philemon

Paul's letter to Philemon stands out as a profound example of Christian love, reconciliation, and intercession. Addressing a personal matter with significant theological implications, Paul crafts his appeal with grace, respect, and strategic persuasion.

Context and Purpose

Paul wrote this letter while imprisoned, likely in Rome around 60-62 C.E. The letter is addressed to Philemon, a wealthy Christian in Colossae, regarding Onesimus, a runaway slave who had become a Christian under Paul's ministry. Paul sends Onesimus back to Philemon with this letter, urging Philemon to receive Onesimus not merely as a slave but as a beloved brother in Christ.

Opening Greetings

Paul begins his letter with a warm and respectful greeting, establishing a tone of affection and respect. He identifies himself as a "prisoner of Christ Jesus" and includes Timothy as a co-sender. This introduction highlights Paul's humility and solidarity with those he addresses.

Philemon 1-3 (UASV): "Paul, a prisoner for Christ Jesus, and Timothy our brother, to Philemon our beloved fellow worker, and Apphia our sister and Archippus our fellow soldier, and the church in your house: Grace to you and peace from God our Father and the Lord Jesus Christ."

Thanksgiving and Prayer

Paul expresses his gratitude for Philemon's love and faith, which have brought joy and encouragement to many believers. This commendation serves to remind Philemon of his Christian duties and character, gently preparing him for the request Paul is about to make.

Philemon 4-7 (UASV): "I thank my God always when I remember you in my prayers, because I hear of your love and of the faith that you have toward the Lord Jesus and for all the saints, and I pray that the sharing of your faith may become effective for the full knowledge of every good thing that is in us for the sake of Christ. For I have derived much joy and comfort from your love, my brother, because the hearts of the saints have been refreshed through you."

Appeal for Onesimus

Paul's appeal on behalf of Onesimus is masterfully constructed. He begins by emphasizing his own position and authority but chooses to appeal based on love rather than command. This approach underscores the transformation in Onesimus and the new relationship between Philemon and Onesimus as brothers in Christ.

Philemon 8-10 (UASV): "Accordingly, though I am bold enough in Christ to command you to do what is required, yet for love's sake I prefer to appeal to you—I, Paul, an old man and now a prisoner also for Christ Jesus—I appeal to you for my child, Onesimus, whose father I became in my imprisonment."

Transformation of Onesimus

Paul highlights the change in Onesimus, who was formerly "useless" but is now "useful" both to Paul and Philemon. This wordplay on the name Onesimus, which means "useful," emphasizes the transformative power of the Gospel.

Philemon 11-12 (UASV): "Formerly he was useless to you, but now he is indeed useful to you and to me. I am sending him back to you, sending my very heart."

Request for Reconciliation

Paul's request is not just for forgiveness but for a redefined relationship. He urges Philemon to welcome Onesimus as he would welcome Paul himself, thus elevating Onesimus's status from a slave to a brother in Christ. This request challenges the social norms and legal expectations of the time, calling Philemon to live out the implications of his faith.

Philemon 15-16 (UASV): "For this perhaps is why he was parted from you for a while, that you might have him back forever, no longer as a bondservant but more than a bondservant, as a beloved brother—especially to me, but how much more to you, both in the flesh and in the Lord."

Paul's Offer to Repay

Paul offers to repay any debt Onesimus owes, reflecting the self-sacrificial love of Christ. This offer also subtly reminds Philemon of the spiritual debt he owes Paul, who brought him to faith.

Philemon 18-19 (UASV): "If he has wronged you at all, or owes you anything, charge that to my account. I, Paul, write this with my own hand: I will repay it—to say nothing of your owing me even your own self."

Closing Remarks and Benediction

Paul concludes with confidence in Philemon's obedience and extends his greetings to the community. This ending reinforces the communal aspect of Christian forgiveness and reconciliation.

Philemon 21-25 (UASV): "Confident of your obedience, I write to you, knowing that you will do even more than I say. At the same time, prepare a guest room for me, for I am hoping that through your prayers I will be graciously given to you. Epaphras, my fellow prisoner in Christ Jesus, sends greetings to you, and so do Mark, Aristarchus, Demas, and Luke, my fellow workers. The grace of the Lord Jesus Christ be with your spirit."

Paul's letter to Philemon is a powerful testament to the principles of Christian love, forgiveness, and reconciliation. It challenges believers to see each other through the lens of their shared faith in Christ, transcending social and cultural barriers. By following Paul's example, Christians today can foster communities characterized by grace and unity, reflecting the transformative power of the Gospel.

Chapter 10: Paul's Theology of Suffering and Perseverance

The apostle Paul offers profound insights into the theology of suffering and perseverance, addressing the hardships and trials that believers face. His letters provide a rich source of encouragement and guidance, helping Christians understand the purpose of suffering and the means to endure it with faith and hope.

The Nature of Christian Suffering

Paul frequently discusses the nature and purpose of suffering in the Christian life. He teaches that suffering is an integral part of following Christ, and it is through these trials that believers are refined and strengthened in their faith.

Romans 5:3-5 (UASV): "Not only that, but we rejoice in our sufferings, knowing that suffering produces endurance, and endurance produces character, and character produces hope, and hope does not put us to shame, because God's love has been poured into our hearts through the Holy Spirit who has been given to us."

Identifying with Christ in Suffering

Paul emphasizes that suffering allows believers to identify with Christ, who endured the ultimate suffering on the cross. This identification is a source of spiritual growth and deeper fellowship with the Savior.

Philippians 3:10-11 (UASV): "That I may know him and the power of his resurrection, and may share his sufferings, becoming like him in his death, that by any means possible I may attain the resurrection from the dead."

The Redemptive Value of Suffering

Paul teaches that suffering has redemptive value, contributing to the believer's sanctification and the spread of the Gospel. Suffering can be a means of demonstrating the power and grace of God, both to the sufferer and to those who witness their faith.

2 Corinthians 4:16-18 (UASV): "So we do not lose heart. Though our outer self is wasting away, our inner self is being renewed day by day. For this light momentary affliction is preparing for us an eternal weight of glory beyond all comparison, as we look not to the things that are seen but to the things that are unseen. For the things that are seen are transient, but the things that are unseen are eternal."

Perseverance Through Faith

Paul's letters are filled with exhortations to persevere in faith despite trials. He encourages believers to maintain their trust in God's promises and to find strength in their relationship with Christ.

Galatians 6:9 (UASV): "And let us not grow weary of doing good, for in due season we will reap, if we do not give up."

The Role of Prayer and the Word

Paul underscores the importance of prayer and the Word of God in enduring suffering. Through prayer, believers find comfort and guidance, and through the Scriptures, they are reminded of God's faithfulness and the ultimate victory in Christ.

Philippians 4:6-7 (UASV): "Do not be anxious about anything, but in everything by prayer and supplication with thanksgiving let your requests be made known to God. And the peace of God, which surpasses all understanding, will guard your hearts and your minds in Christ Jesus."

Romans 15:4 (UASV): "For whatever was written in former days was written for our instruction, that through endurance and the encouragement of the Scriptures we might have hope."

Community Support

Paul highlights the importance of the Christian community in providing support and encouragement during times of suffering. Believers are called to bear one another's burdens and to offer practical and spiritual support.

Galatians 6:2 (UASV): "Bear one another's burdens, and so fulfill the law of Christ."

2 Corinthians 1:3-4 (UASV): "Blessed be the God and Father of our Lord Jesus Christ, the Father of mercies and God of all comfort, who comforts us in all our affliction, so that we may be able to comfort those who are in any affliction, with the comfort with which we ourselves are comforted by God."

The Example of Paul's Own Suffering

Paul often references his own experiences of suffering to illustrate his teachings and to encourage others. His perseverance through numerous trials serves as a powerful testimony to the sustaining power of God's grace.

2 Corinthians 11:24-28 (UASV): "Five times I received at the hands of the Jews the forty lashes less one. Three times I was beaten with rods. Once I was stoned. Three times I was shipwrecked; a night and a day I was adrift at sea; on frequent journeys, in danger from rivers, danger from robbers, danger from my own people, danger from Gentiles, danger in the city, danger in the wilderness, danger at sea, danger from false brothers; in toil and hardship, through many a sleepless night, in hunger and thirst, often without food, in cold and exposure. And, apart from other things, there is the daily pressure on me of my anxiety for all the churches."

The Ultimate Hope

Paul's theology of suffering is anchored in the ultimate hope of resurrection and eternal life. He assures believers that their present sufferings are temporary and that they will be fully redeemed and glorified with Christ.

Romans 8:18 (UASV): "For I consider that the sufferings of this present time are not worth comparing with the glory that is to be revealed to us."

1 Corinthians 15:54-55 (UASV): "When the perishable puts on the imperishable, and the mortal puts on immortality, then shall come to pass the saying that is written: 'Death is swallowed up in victory. O death, where is your victory? O death, where is your sting?'"

By embracing Paul's teachings on suffering and perseverance, modern Christians can find strength and encouragement to endure trials with faith, knowing that their suffering has purpose and that their hope in Christ is secure. This understanding transforms suffering into an opportunity for spiritual growth and a deeper relationship with God.

Chapter 11: Paul's Vision of Unity in the Body of Christ

The apostle Paul fervently advocated for unity within the body of Christ, emphasizing that all believers, regardless of their backgrounds, are one in Jesus. This chapter delves into Paul's vision of unity, exploring his teachings on the importance of harmony, the role of diversity within unity, and the practical steps for achieving and maintaining this unity in the church.

The Basis of Unity in Christ

Paul's letters consistently highlight that the foundation of Christian unity is Jesus Christ. He stresses that believers are united through their common faith in Christ and their shared experience of salvation. This unity transcends ethnic, social, and cultural differences, creating a new, harmonious community of believers.

Ephesians 4:4-6 (UASV): "There is one body and one Spirit—just as you were called to the one hope that belongs to your call—one Lord, one faith, one baptism, one God and Father of all, who is over all and through all and in all."

The Role of the Holy Spirit

The Holy Spirit plays a crucial role in fostering unity among believers. Paul teaches that the Spirit indwells each believer, guiding them into all truth and enabling them to live in harmony with one another. The Spirit's work in the hearts of believers produces the fruit of love, joy, peace, patience, kindness, goodness, faithfulness, gentleness, and self-control, which are essential for maintaining unity.

1 Corinthians 12:13 (UASV): "For in one Spirit we were all baptized into one body—Jews or Greeks, slaves or free—and all were made to drink of one Spirit."

Unity in the Body of Christ

Paul acknowledges and emphasizes the unity within the body of Christ. He teaches that each believer is given different gifts and roles, all of which are necessary for the health and function of the church. This variety of gifts, far from being a source of division, is intended to strengthen the church and help it fulfill its mission.

Romans 12:4-6 (UASV): "For as in one body we have many members, and the members do not all have the same function, so we, though many, are one body in Christ, and individually members one of another. Having gifts that differ according to the grace given to us, let us use them."

1 Corinthians 12:18-20 (UASV): "But as it is, God arranged the members in the body, each one of them, as he chose. If all were a single member, where would the body be? As it is, there are many parts, yet one body."

Paul's teaching underscores that the unity of the church is rooted in the harmonious functioning of its members, each contributing uniquely according to the grace given by God. This unity ensures the effective ministry and witness of the church in the world.

The Call to Live in Harmony

Paul exhorts believers to live in harmony with one another, reflecting the unity they have in Christ. He emphasizes the importance of humility, gentleness, patience, and bearing with one another in love. These qualities help to maintain the unity of the Spirit and foster a peaceful and supportive community.

Ephesians 4:1-3 (UASV): "I therefore, a prisoner for the Lord, urge you to walk in a manner worthy of the calling to which you have been called, with all humility and gentleness, with patience, bearing with one another in love, eager to maintain the unity of the Spirit in the bond of peace."

Overcoming Divisions

Paul addresses various divisions within the early church, urging believers to put aside their differences and focus on their common faith in Christ. He confronts issues of ethnic, social, and theological divisions, calling for reconciliation and unity.

Galatians 3:28 (UASV): "There is neither Jew nor Greek, there is neither slave nor free, there is no male and female, for you are all one in Christ Jesus."

1 Corinthians 1:10 (UASV): "I appeal to you, brothers, by the name of our Lord Jesus Christ, that all of you agree, and that there be no divisions among you, but that you be united in the same mind and the same judgment."

Practical Steps for Unity

Paul provides practical advice for achieving and maintaining unity within the church. He encourages believers to practice love, forgiveness, and mutual respect. He also emphasizes the importance of addressing conflicts promptly and seeking reconciliation.

Colossians 3:12-14 (UASV): "Put on then, as God's chosen ones, holy and beloved, compassionate hearts, kindness, humility, meekness, and patience, bearing with one another and, if one has a complaint against another, forgiving each other; as the Lord has forgiven you, so you also must forgive. And above all these put on love, which binds everything together in perfect harmony."

Philippians 2:2-4 (UASV): "Complete my joy by being of the same mind, having the same love, being in full accord and of one mind. Do nothing from selfish ambition or conceit, but in humility count others more significant than yourselves. Let each of you look not only to his own interests, but also to the interests of others."

Unity in Worship and Service

Paul underscores the importance of unity in worship and service. He teaches that believers are to come together to worship God and serve one another, reflecting the unity of the body of Christ. This communal worship and service strengthen the bonds between believers and help to maintain the unity of the church.

Romans 15:5-6 (UASV): "May the God of endurance and encouragement grant you to live in such harmony with one another, in accord with Christ Jesus, that together you may with one voice glorify the God and Father of our Lord Jesus Christ."

1 Corinthians 14:26 (UASV): "What then, brothers? When you come together, each one has a hymn, a lesson, a revelation, a tongue, or an interpretation. Let all things be done for building up."

The Example of Christ

Paul frequently points to the example of Christ as the ultimate model for unity. Jesus' selfless love, humility, and obedience to the Father serve as the standard for all believers. By following Christ's example, believers can foster unity within the church and reflect the love of God to the world.

Philippians 2:5-8 (UASV): "Have this mind among yourselves, which is yours in Christ Jesus, who, though he was in the form of God, did not count equality with God a thing to be grasped, but emptied himself, by taking the form of a servant, being born in the likeness of men. And being found in human form, he humbled himself by becoming obedient to the point of death, even death on a cross."

The Witness of Unity

Paul teaches that the unity of the church serves as a powerful witness to the world. When believers live in harmony and love, they reflect the unity of the Godhead and demonstrate the transformative power of the Gospel. This witness attracts others to the faith and glorifies God.

John 17:21 (UASV): "That they may all be one, just as you, Father, are in me, and I in you, that they also may be in us, so that the world may believe that you have sent me."

Ephesians 2:19-22 (UASV): "So then you are no longer strangers and aliens, but you are fellow citizens with the saints and members of the household of God, built on the foundation of the apostles and prophets, Christ Jesus himself being the cornerstone, in whom the whole structure, being joined together, grows into a holy temple in the Lord. In him you also are being built together into a dwelling place for God by the Spirit."

By embracing Paul's teachings on unity, modern Christians can work towards creating harmonious and loving communities that reflect the heart of God. This unity not only strengthens the church but also serves as a compelling testimony to the power of the Gospel in transforming lives and relationships. Through love, humility, and mutual respect, believers can maintain the unity of the Spirit and fulfill their calling as the body of Christ.

Chapter 12: Paul's Mentorship of Timothy

The relationship between the apostle Paul and Timothy offers a profound example of Christian mentorship and discipleship. This chapter explores how Paul met Timothy, how he trained and prepared him for ministry, and the lasting impact of their relationship on the early church and Christian leadership.

Meeting Timothy

Paul first met Timothy during his second missionary journey. Timothy was a young disciple from Lystra, whose mother was a Jewish believer and whose father was a Greek. Timothy's mixed heritage made him a unique and valuable companion for Paul's mission to both Jews and Gentiles.

Acts 16:1-3 (UASV): "Paul came also to Derbe and to Lystra. A disciple was there, named Timothy, the son of a Jewish woman who was a believer, but his father was a Greek. He was well spoken of by the brothers at Lystra and Iconium. Paul wanted Timothy to accompany him, and he took him and circumcised him because of the Jews who were in those places, for they all knew that his father was a Greek."

Paul saw great potential in Timothy and chose him to accompany him on his journeys. This decision was likely influenced by the positive reports Paul received about Timothy's faith and character from the believers in Lystra and Iconium.

Timothy's Background and Faith

Timothy's strong faith was nurtured from a young age by his mother, Eunice, and his grandmother, Lois. Paul acknowledges their influence in his letters, highlighting the importance of a godly upbringing and the role of family in spiritual formation.

2 Timothy 1:5 (UASV): "I am reminded of your sincere faith, a faith that dwelt first in your grandmother Lois and your mother Eunice and now, I am sure, dwells in you as well."

This foundation of faith made Timothy an ideal candidate for ministry. His upbringing in a devout Jewish-Christian household equipped him with a deep understanding of the Scriptures, which was crucial for his future role as a church leader.

Training and Mentoring

Paul took Timothy under his wing, providing him with practical ministry experience and theological training. Timothy accompanied Paul on his missionary journeys, witnessing firsthand the challenges and triumphs of evangelistic work. This hands-on training was invaluable in preparing Timothy for his future responsibilities.

1 Corinthians 4:17 (UASV): "That is why I sent you Timothy, my beloved and faithful child in the Lord, to remind you of my ways in Christ, as I teach them everywhere in every church."

Paul's letters to Timothy, known as the Pastoral Epistles, offer further insight into the mentorship relationship. These letters are filled with personal advice, theological instruction, and encouragement, reflecting Paul's deep concern for Timothy's spiritual growth and effectiveness in ministry.

Paul's Instructions to Timothy

Paul's instructions to Timothy cover various aspects of ministry, including leadership, teaching, and personal conduct. He emphasizes the importance of sound doctrine, urging Timothy to guard the truth of the Gospel and to teach it faithfully.

1 Timothy 4:6-8 (UASV): "If you put these things before the brothers, you will be a good servant of Christ Jesus, being trained in the words of the faith and of the good doctrine that you have followed. Have nothing to do with irreverent, silly myths. Rather train yourself for godliness; for while bodily training is of some value, godliness is of

value in every way, as it holds promise for the present life and also for the life to come."

Paul also addresses the challenges of leadership, encouraging Timothy to be a strong and courageous leader, even in the face of opposition and difficulty.

2 Timothy 1:6-7 (UASV): "For this reason I remind you to fan into flame the gift of God, which is in you through the laying on of my hands, for God gave us a spirit not of fear but of power and love and self-control."

Preparing Timothy for Leadership

Paul's mentorship was aimed at preparing Timothy to take on significant leadership roles within the church. He entrusted Timothy with important tasks, such as overseeing the church in Ephesus and addressing doctrinal issues and false teachings.

1 Timothy 1:3 (UASV): "As I urged you when I was going to Macedonia, remain at Ephesus so that you may charge certain persons not to teach any different doctrine."

Paul also provided Timothy with practical advice on how to handle various situations within the church, from dealing with elders and widows to managing his own personal conduct and spiritual life.

1 Timothy 5:21-22 (UASV): "In the presence of God and of Christ Jesus and of the elect angels, I charge you to keep these rules without prejudging, doing nothing from partiality. Do not be hasty in the laying on of hands, nor take part in the sins of others; keep yourself pure."

Encouragement and Support

Throughout his letters, Paul consistently encourages and supports Timothy, reminding him of his calling and the gifts God has given him. This encouragement was crucial for Timothy, who faced significant challenges and opposition in his ministry.

2 Timothy 4:1-2 (UASV): "I charge you in the presence of God and of Christ Jesus, who is to judge the living and the dead, and by his

appearing and his kingdom: preach the word; be ready in season and out of season; reprove, rebuke, and exhort, with complete patience and teaching."

Paul's affirmation of Timothy's abilities and his constant reminders of God's faithfulness helped to bolster Timothy's confidence and resolve, enabling him to persevere in his ministry.

The Legacy of Paul's Mentorship

The relationship between Paul and Timothy serves as a model for Christian mentorship and discipleship. Paul's investment in Timothy's life had a lasting impact, not only on Timothy himself but also on the churches he served and the generations of believers who followed.

Paul's mentorship underscores the importance of investing in the next generation of leaders, providing them with the training, support, and encouragement they need to fulfill their God-given callings. By following Paul's example, modern Christians can help to ensure the continued growth and health of the church.

2 Timothy 2:2 (UASV): "And what you have heard from me in the presence of many witnesses entrust to faithful men who will be able to teach others also."

By examining the relationship between Paul and Timothy, believers today can glean valuable lessons on mentorship, leadership, and the importance of nurturing the faith and gifts of others. This dynamic partnership demonstrates the transformative power of discipleship and the enduring impact of investing in the spiritual growth of others. Through such relationships, the church continues to grow and thrive, fulfilling its mission to spread the Gospel and make disciples of all nations.

Chapter 13: Paul and His Many Traveling Companions

The apostle Paul's ministry was marked by his collaboration with numerous fellow workers who played crucial roles in his evangelistic efforts and church-planting missions. These companions provided support, shared in the hardships, and contributed significantly to the spread of the Gospel. This chapter explores some of the major figures who traveled and worked alongside Paul, highlighting their contributions and the impact they had on the early Christian movement.

Barnabas: The Encourager

Barnabas, whose name means "son of encouragement," was one of the earliest and most significant companions of Paul. He was instrumental in introducing Paul to the apostles in Jerusalem after Paul's dramatic conversion. Barnabas was known for his generous spirit and willingness to support new believers.

Acts 11:22-24 (UASV): "The report of this came to the ears of the church in Jerusalem, and they sent Barnabas to Antioch. When he came and saw the grace of God, he was glad, and he exhorted them all to remain faithful to the Lord with steadfast purpose, for he was a good man, full of the Holy Spirit and of faith. And a great many people were added to the Lord."

Barnabas and Paul worked closely together on Paul's first missionary journey, planting churches and spreading the Gospel. Their partnership was pivotal in the early expansion of Christianity, particularly among Gentiles.

Silas: The Faithful Partner

Silas, also known as Silvanus, joined Paul after the disagreement between Paul and Barnabas. Silas was a prominent leader in the early church and accompanied Paul on his second missionary journey. He was known for his steadfast faith and resilience, particularly during times of persecution.

Acts 16:25-26 (UASV): "About midnight Paul and Silas were praying and singing hymns to God, and the prisoners were listening to them, and suddenly there was a great earthquake, so that the foundations of the prison were shaken. And immediately all the doors were opened, and everyone's bonds were unfastened."

Silas played a crucial role in establishing and strengthening churches, especially in Philippi, Thessalonica, and Berea. His partnership with Paul exemplified the importance of collaboration and mutual support in ministry.

Timothy: The Loyal Disciple

Timothy, a young disciple from Lystra, became one of Paul's closest companions and most trusted co-workers. Paul saw great potential in Timothy and invested significantly in his training and development. Timothy accompanied Paul on his journeys and was later entrusted with significant leadership responsibilities.

Philippians 2:19-22 (UASV): "I hope in the Lord Jesus to send Timothy to you soon, so that I too may be cheered by news of you. For I have no one like him, who will be genuinely concerned for your welfare. For they all seek their own interests, not those of Jesus Christ. But you know Timothy's proven worth, how as a son with a father he has served with me in the gospel."

Timothy's role included overseeing the church in Ephesus and addressing doctrinal and pastoral issues. His relationship with Paul highlights the importance of mentorship and the impact of investing in the next generation of leaders.

Luke: The Beloved Physician

Luke, the author of the Gospel of Luke and the Acts of the Apostles, was a loyal companion and meticulous historian. As a physician, Luke likely provided physical and medical support to Paul, who endured numerous hardships and ailments.

Colossians 4:14 (UASV): "Luke the beloved physician greets you, as does Demas."

Luke's detailed accounts in Acts provide invaluable insights into the early church and Paul's missionary journeys. His dedication to documenting the spread of the Gospel and the growth of the church has left a lasting legacy for future generations of believers.

Titus: The Trusted Delegate

Titus was another significant co-worker of Paul, known for his reliability and ability to handle challenging situations. Paul entrusted Titus with important missions, such as addressing issues in the church in Corinth and organizing the collection for the poor in Jerusalem.

2 Corinthians 8:16-17 (UASV): "But thanks be to God, who put into the heart of Titus the same earnest care I have for you. For he not only accepted our appeal, but being himself very earnest, he is going to you of his own accord."

Titus's role as a mediator and organizer highlights the importance of administrative and pastoral skills in church leadership. His work ensured the smooth functioning and unity of the early Christian communities.

Priscilla and Aquila: The Hospitable Teachers

Priscilla and Aquila, a married couple, were notable for their hospitality, teaching, and leadership within the early church. They first met Paul in Corinth, where they worked together as tentmakers. Their home served as a center for Christian fellowship and teaching.

Acts 18:24-26 (UASV): "Now a Jew named Apollos, a native of Alexandria, came to Ephesus. He was an eloquent man, competent in the Scriptures. He had been instructed in the way of the Lord. And being fervent in spirit, he spoke and taught accurately the things concerning Jesus, though he knew only the baptism of John. He began to speak boldly in the synagogue, but when Priscilla and Aquila heard him, they took him aside and explained to him the way of God more accurately."

Priscilla and Aquila's mentorship of Apollos is a prime example of their dedication to teaching and their commitment to nurturing other leaders in the faith.

Epaphroditus: The Devoted Worker

Epaphroditus was a dedicated worker who served alongside Paul, particularly in Philippi. He was sent by the Philippian church to support Paul during his imprisonment in Rome. Epaphroditus's service was marked by his willingness to endure hardship and his deep concern for the well-being of the church.

Philippians 2:25-30 (UASV): "I have thought it necessary to send to you Epaphroditus my brother and fellow worker and fellow soldier, and your messenger and minister to my need, for he has been longing for you all and has been distressed because you heard that he was ill. Indeed he was ill, near to death. But God had mercy on him, and not only on him but on me also, lest I should have sorrow upon sorrow. I am the more eager to send him, therefore, that you may rejoice at seeing him again, and that I may be less anxious. So receive him in the Lord with all joy, and honor such men, for he nearly died for the work of Christ, risking his life to complete what was lacking in your service to me."

Epaphroditus's example underscores the importance of sacrificial service and the profound impact of dedicated workers in supporting and advancing the ministry.

Paul's many traveling companions were vital to his ministry and the spread of the Gospel. Each played a unique role, contributing their gifts, skills, and dedication to the mission. Their examples highlight the importance of collaboration, mentorship, and mutual support in Christian ministry. By working together, they helped to establish and strengthen the early church, leaving a lasting legacy for future generations of believers. In the next chapter, we will explore some of the lesser-known companions of Paul, whose contributions, though often overlooked, were equally significant in the spread of the Gospel.

Chapter 14: Paul's Lesser-Known Fellow Workers

In addition to the prominent figures who traveled and worked alongside Paul, there were numerous lesser-known companions who played crucial roles in his ministry. These individuals, though not as widely recognized, contributed significantly to the spread of the Gospel and the establishment of early Christian communities. This chapter highlights some of these faithful workers, exploring their contributions and the impact they had on Paul's mission.

Asyncritus: The Unifying Worker

Asyncritus is mentioned briefly in Paul's letter to the Romans. Although little is known about him, his inclusion in Paul's greetings suggests that he was a valued member of the Christian community in Rome.

Romans 16:14 (UASV): "Greet Asyncritus, Phlegon, Hermes, Patrobas, Hermas, and the brothers who are with them."

Asyncritus, along with others mentioned, likely played a role in fostering unity and strengthening the fellowship among believers in Rome. His mention indicates the importance of every member's contribution to the church's overall health and unity.

Hermas: The Faithful Servant

Hermas is another lesser-known companion greeted by Paul in Romans. His inclusion in Paul's letter highlights his role in the early church, possibly as a leader or a servant within the Christian community.

Romans 16:14 (UASV): "Greet Asyncritus, Phlegon, Hermes, Patrobas, Hermas, and the brothers who are with them."

Although details about Hermas's specific contributions are scarce, his presence in Paul's greetings underscores the value of every faithful servant in the body of Christ.

Julia: The Esteemed Sister

Julia is one of the few women mentioned by Paul in his letters, indicating her significant role within the early Christian community. Her mention alongside other prominent figures suggests that she was highly regarded and respected among the believers.

Romans 16:15 (UASV): "Greet Philologus, Julia, Nereus and his sister, and Olympas, and all the saints who are with them."

Julia's inclusion highlights the important role of women in the early church, serving as a reminder of the diverse contributions of both men and women in advancing the Gospel.

Philologus: The Knowledgeable Brother

Philologus, whose name means "lover of the word," is mentioned by Paul in his greetings to the Roman believers. This name may indicate his dedication to studying and teaching the Scriptures, contributing to the spiritual growth of the community.

Romans 16:15 (UASV): "Greet Philologus, Julia, Nereus and his sister, and Olympas, and all the saints who are with them."

Philologus's role likely involved teaching and encouraging the believers, emphasizing the importance of sound doctrine and the study of God's Word.

Tychicus: The Faithful Messenger

Tychicus was a trusted companion and messenger for Paul, often tasked with delivering letters and providing updates to various churches. His role as a courier was crucial in maintaining communication between Paul and the early Christian communities.

Ephesians 6:21-22 (UASV): "So that you also may know how I am and what I am doing, Tychicus the beloved brother and faithful minister in the Lord will tell you everything. I have sent him to you for this very purpose, that you may know how we are, and that he may encourage your hearts."

Tychicus's reliability and dedication made him an invaluable asset to Paul's ministry, ensuring that important messages and instructions were conveyed accurately and promptly.

Epaphras: The Dedicated Intercessor

Epaphras, a native of Colossae, was instrumental in establishing and nurturing the church there. He was known for his fervent prayers and deep concern for the spiritual well-being of the believers.

Colossians 4:12-13 (UASV): "Epaphras, who is one of you, a servant of Christ Jesus, greets you, always struggling on your behalf in his prayers, that you may stand mature and fully assured in all the will of God. For I bear him witness that he has worked hard for you and for those in Laodicea and in Hierapolis."

Epaphras's commitment to prayer and pastoral care highlights the vital role of intercessors and shepherds within the church, tirelessly working for the growth and maturity of the congregation.

Aristarchus: The Loyal Companion

Aristarchus was a Macedonian from Thessalonica who accompanied Paul on several of his journeys, including his voyage to Rome as a prisoner. His willingness to endure hardship and danger alongside Paul demonstrates his deep commitment to the ministry.

Acts 19:29 (UASV): "So the city was filled with the confusion, and they rushed together into the theater, dragging with them Gaius and Aristarchus, Macedonians who were Paul's companions in travel."

Colossians 4:10 (UASV): "Aristarchus my fellow prisoner greets you, and Mark the cousin of Barnabas (concerning whom you have received instructions—if he comes to you, welcome him)."

Aristarchus's loyalty and steadfastness were a source of strength and encouragement to Paul, exemplifying the importance of faithful companions in ministry.

Crescens: The Missionary to Galatia

Crescens is briefly mentioned by Paul in his second letter to Timothy, indicating that he was sent on a mission to Galatia. This suggests that Crescens was entrusted with significant responsibilities in spreading the Gospel and supporting the churches in that region.

2 Timothy 4:10 (UASV): "For Demas, in love with this present world, has deserted me and gone to Thessalonica. Crescens has gone to Galatia, Titus to Dalmatia."

Crescens's mention highlights the ongoing efforts of Paul's companions to carry on the work of evangelism and church planting in various regions.

Carpus: The Hospitable Host

Carpus is mentioned by Paul in his final letter to Timothy, where Paul requests that Timothy bring his cloak, books, and parchments that were left with Carpus in Troas. This indicates that Carpus was a trusted host who provided Paul with a place to stay and safeguarded his belongings.

2 Timothy 4:13 (UASV): "When you come, bring the cloak that I left with Carpus at Troas, also the books, and above all the parchments."

Carpus's hospitality and support reflect the essential role of those who provide practical assistance and resources to traveling missionaries and leaders.

Erastus: The City Treasurer

Erastus is identified as the city treasurer of Corinth, indicating that he held a prominent and influential position. His support for Paul's ministry demonstrates the diverse backgrounds of those who contributed to the early church.

Romans 16:23 (UASV): "Gaius, who is host to me and to the whole church, greets you. Erastus, the city treasurer, and our brother Quartus, greet you."

Erastus's involvement illustrates the importance of believers using their positions and resources to further the work of the Gospel.

Theodotus: The Compassionate Caregiver

Theodotus is another lesser-known companion who is mentioned in the early Christian writings. Though not explicitly mentioned in Paul's letters, his role as a caregiver and supporter of the apostles highlights the significance of compassionate service within the Christian community.

While details about Theodotus are limited, his dedication to caring for the needs of others and supporting the ministry of the apostles serves as a reminder of the diverse ways in which believers can contribute to the spread of the Gospel.

These lesser-known companions of Paul played indispensable roles in his ministry, each contributing their unique gifts and resources to the advancement of the Gospel. Their examples underscore the importance of every believer's contribution to the mission of the church, regardless of their prominence or recognition. By working together in unity and dedication, they helped to establish and strengthen the early Christian communities, laying a foundation for the continued growth and spread of the faith. In the next chapter, we will examine those companions who fell away from the faith, exploring the challenges and lessons their accounts offer for believers today.

Chapter 15: Those Who Fell Away: Lessons from Alexander, Demas, Hermogenes, and Phygelus

While the apostle Paul was blessed with many faithful companions who supported his ministry, there were also those who fell away from the faith. The stories of Alexander, Demas, Hermogenes, and Phygelus serve as sobering reminders of the challenges and temptations that can lead believers astray. By examining their failures, we can learn valuable lessons to help us remain steadfast in our own faith.

Alexander: The Adversary of the Faith

Alexander is mentioned twice in Paul's letters, and both references highlight his opposition to the Gospel. In 1 Timothy, Paul warns Timothy about Alexander, indicating that he had rejected the faith and caused significant harm.

1 Timothy 1:19-20 (UASV): "Holding faith and a good conscience. By rejecting this, some have made shipwreck of their faith, among whom are Hymenaeus and Alexander, whom I have handed over to Satan that they may learn not to blaspheme."

Later, in 2 Timothy, Paul recounts the personal harm Alexander had done to him, further emphasizing the danger posed by his actions.

2 Timothy 4:14-15 (UASV): "Alexander the coppersmith did me great harm; the Lord will repay him according to his deeds. Beware of him yourself, for he strongly opposed our message."

Lessons from Alexander's Fall

Alexander's fall serves as a warning against rejecting the faith and actively opposing the Gospel. To avoid such a fate, believers must:

1. **Maintain a Firm Foundation in the Faith**: Regular study of the Scriptures and sound teaching helps to build a strong foundation that can withstand false teachings and temptations.
2. **Guard Against Pride and Bitterness**: Pride and unresolved bitterness can lead to a hardening of the heart and a rejection of the faith. Humility and forgiveness are essential in maintaining a healthy spiritual life.
3. **Stay Vigilant Against False Teachings**: Believers must be discerning and alert to false teachings that can lead them away from the truth of the Gospel.

Demas: The Lover of This World

Demas is mentioned in three of Paul's letters, initially as a faithful companion but later as one who abandoned Paul and the faith. In Colossians and Philemon, Demas is listed among Paul's fellow workers, indicating his active involvement in the ministry.

Colossians 4:14 (UASV): "Luke the beloved physician greets you, as does Demas."

Philemon 1:24 (UASV): "And so do Mark, Aristarchus, Demas, and Luke, my fellow workers."

However, in 2 Timothy, Paul laments Demas's departure, attributing it to his love for the present world.

2 Timothy 4:10 (UASV): "For Demas, in love with this present world, has deserted me and gone to Thessalonica. Crescens has gone to Galatia, Titus to Dalmatia."

Lessons from Demas's Fall

Demas's fall highlights the dangers of worldly attachments and distractions. To avoid falling away like Demas, believers should:

1. **Keep Eternal Perspective**: Focusing on eternal rewards rather than temporary pleasures helps to maintain faithfulness.

Colossians 3:2 (UASV) says, "Set your minds on things that are above, not on things that are on earth."

2. **Cultivate Contentment**: Learning to be content with what God provides helps to guard against the lure of materialism and the love of the world.

3. **Stay Committed to Fellowship**: Remaining actively involved in Christian fellowship provides accountability and encouragement, helping to prevent drifting away from the faith.

Hermogenes and Phygelus: The Deserters

Hermogenes and Phygelus are mentioned only once in Paul's letters, in a context that highlights their desertion. Paul expresses sorrow over their abandonment, indicating that they, along with others, had turned away from him during a time of great need.

2 Timothy 1:15 (UASV): "You are aware that all who are in Asia turned away from me, among whom are Phygelus and Hermogenes."

Their departure likely added to Paul's suffering and loneliness during his imprisonment.

Lessons from Hermogenes and Phygelus's Fall

The example of Hermogenes and Phygelus teaches us the importance of steadfast loyalty and courage in the face of adversity. To avoid falling away like them, believers should:

1. **Develop Resilience**: Building spiritual resilience through prayer, Scripture study, and fellowship helps to withstand trials and challenges.

2. **Stand Firm in Persecution**: Understanding that persecution is a part of the Christian life and preparing mentally and spiritually to endure it helps to prevent falling away.

3. **Support Fellow Believers**: Being a source of support and encouragement to others, especially during difficult times, helps to build a strong and united body of Christ.

Conclusion: Learning from Their Mistakes

The stories of Alexander, Demas, Hermogenes, and Phygelus remind us of the real dangers and challenges that can lead believers astray. By learning from their mistakes, we can take proactive steps to safeguard our faith and remain steadfast in our commitment to Christ. This involves maintaining a firm foundation in the faith, guarding against pride and worldly attachments, developing resilience, and supporting one another in the body of Christ.

Hebrews 3:12-14 (UASV) offers a fitting exhortation: "Take care, brothers, lest there be in any of you an evil, unbelieving heart, leading you to fall away from the living God. But exhort one another every day, as long as it is called 'today,' that none of you may be hardened by the deceitfulness of sin. For we have come to share in Christ, if indeed we hold our original confidence firm to the end."

By heeding these lessons, we can strive to finish the race faithfully, as Paul himself did, and receive the crown of righteousness promised to all who love Christ's appearing.

Chapter 16: Paul's First Missionary Journey

Paul's first missionary journey marks a significant chapter in the spread of early Christianity. This journey, undertaken with Barnabas, began a series of missions that would establish Paul as a leading apostle to the Gentiles and lay the groundwork for the expansion of the Christian faith. This chapter provides an in-depth exploration of the events, challenges, and successes of Paul's first missionary journey, highlighting key locations, encounters, and the theological implications of his work.

The Commissioning at Antioch

The journey begins in Antioch, a prominent city in Syria and an early center of Christian activity. It was here that the Holy Spirit directed the church to set apart Paul and Barnabas for the work to which they were called.

Acts 13:2-3 (UASV): "While they were worshiping the Lord and fasting, the Holy Spirit said, 'Set apart for me Barnabas and Saul for the work to which I have called them.' Then after fasting and praying they laid their hands on them and sent them off."

This commissioning highlights the importance of prayer, fasting, and the leading of the Holy Spirit in missionary work. It also underscores the supportive role of the local church in sending out and supporting missionaries.

Cyprus: Preaching in Salamis and Paphos

Paul and Barnabas first sailed to Cyprus, accompanied by John Mark. They began their ministry in Salamis, preaching the Word of God in the Jewish synagogues. This strategy of starting in the synagogues would become a hallmark of Paul's approach, reflecting his initial focus on reaching his fellow Jews.

Acts 13:4-5 (UASV): "So, being sent out by the Holy Spirit, they went down to Seleucia, and from there they sailed to Cyprus. When they arrived at Salamis, they proclaimed the word of God in the synagogues of the Jews. And they had John to assist them."

In Paphos, they encountered a significant challenge in the form of Elymas the magician, who opposed their message. Paul, filled with the Holy Spirit, rebuked Elymas, resulting in his temporary blindness. This miracle led to the conversion of the proconsul, Sergius Paulus, demonstrating the power of God and the authority of Paul's apostolic mission.

Acts 13:9-12 (UASV): "But Saul, who was also called Paul, filled with the Holy Spirit, looked intently at him and said, 'You son of the devil, you enemy of all righteousness, full of all deceit and villainy, will you not stop making crooked the straight paths of the Lord? And now, behold, the hand of the Lord is upon you, and you will be blind and unable to see the sun for a time.' Immediately mist and darkness fell upon him, and he went about seeking people to lead him by the hand. Then the proconsul believed, when he saw what had occurred, for he was astonished at the teaching of the Lord."

Perga and Pisidian Antioch

After leaving Cyprus, Paul and his companions traveled to Perga in Pamphylia. It was here that John Mark left them to return to Jerusalem, an event that later caused a significant rift between Paul and Barnabas.

Acts 13:13 (UASV): "Now Paul and his companions set sail from Paphos and came to Perga in Pamphylia. And John left them and returned to Jerusalem."

From Perga, Paul and Barnabas traveled to Pisidian Antioch, where Paul delivered a powerful sermon in the synagogue. He recounted the history of Israel, culminating in the proclamation of Jesus as the promised Savior. This sermon emphasizes the continuity of God's redemptive plan from the Old Testament to the coming of Christ.

Acts 13:32-33 (UASV): "And we bring you the good news that what God promised to the fathers, this he has fulfilled to us their children by raising Jesus, as also it is written in the second Psalm, 'You are my Son, today I have begotten you.'"

Paul's message received mixed reactions. While many Gentiles eagerly embraced the Gospel, some Jews were filled with jealousy and opposed Paul and Barnabas, leading to their expulsion from the city.

Acts 13:45-46 (UASV): "But when the Jews saw the crowds, they were filled with jealousy and began to contradict what was spoken by Paul, reviling him. And Paul and Barnabas spoke out boldly, saying, 'It was necessary that the word of God be spoken first to you. Since you thrust it aside and judge yourselves unworthy of eternal life, behold, we are turning to the Gentiles.'"

Iconium: Division and Perseverance

Paul and Barnabas next traveled to Iconium, where they again began by preaching in the synagogue. Their message led to a division among the people, with some supporting the apostles and others opposing them. Despite the opposition, Paul and Barnabas remained in Iconium for a significant period, boldly proclaiming the Gospel and performing miracles.

Acts 14:1-3 (UASV): "Now at Iconium they entered together into the Jewish synagogue and spoke in such a way that a great number of both Jews and Greeks believed. But the unbelieving Jews stirred up the Gentiles and poisoned their minds against the brothers. So they remained for a long time, speaking boldly for the Lord, who bore witness to the word of his grace, granting signs and wonders to be done by their hands."

Eventually, the opposition grew so fierce that a plot to stone them forced Paul and Barnabas to flee to Lystra and Derbe.

Lystra and Derbe: Miracles and Persecution

In Lystra, Paul healed a man who had been lame from birth, leading the people to believe that Paul and Barnabas were gods. They called Barnabas Zeus and Paul Hermes and attempted to offer sacrifices to them. Paul and Barnabas vehemently rejected this, insisting that they were merely human and urging the people to turn to the living God.

Acts 14:14-15 (UASV): "But when the apostles Barnabas and Paul heard of it, they tore their garments and rushed out into the crowd, crying out, 'Men, why are you doing these things? We also are men, of like nature with you, and we bring you good news, that you should turn from these vain things to a living God, who made the heaven and the earth and the sea and all that is in them.'"

Despite their efforts, some Jews from Antioch and Iconium arrived and turned the crowd against them. Paul was stoned and left for dead, but he miraculously survived and continued his ministry.

Acts 14:19-20 (UASV): "But Jews came from Antioch and Iconium, and having persuaded the crowds, they stoned Paul and dragged him out of the city, supposing that he was dead. But when the disciples gathered about him, he rose up and entered the city, and on the next day he went on with Barnabas to Derbe."

In Derbe, Paul and Barnabas made many disciples, demonstrating the resilience and determination that characterized their missionary efforts.

Returning to Strengthen the Churches

After their work in Derbe, Paul and Barnabas retraced their steps, returning to Lystra, Iconium, and Antioch to strengthen the disciples and appoint elders in each church. They encouraged the believers to remain steadfast in their faith despite the hardships they would face.

Acts 14:21-23 (UASV): "When they had preached the gospel to that city and had made many disciples, they returned to Lystra and to

Iconium and to Antioch, strengthening the souls of the disciples, encouraging them to continue in the faith, and saying that through many tribulations we must enter the kingdom of God. And when they had appointed elders for them in every church, with prayer and fasting they committed them to the Lord in whom they had believed."

Reporting Back to Antioch

Upon completing their journey, Paul and Barnabas returned to Antioch in Syria, where they reported all that God had done through them and how He had opened a door of faith to the Gentiles.

Acts 14:26-27 (UASV): "And from there they sailed to Antioch, where they had been commended to the grace of God for the work that they had fulfilled. And when they arrived and gathered the church together, they declared all that God had done with them, and how he had opened a door of faith to the Gentiles."

Paul's first missionary journey was a groundbreaking endeavor that established the foundation for the rapid spread of Christianity among Gentile populations. The journey was marked by significant successes, fierce opposition, and miraculous events, all of which demonstrated God's power and faithfulness in advancing His kingdom. This journey set the stage for Paul's subsequent missions and the continued growth of the early church.

Chapter 17: Paul's Second Missionary Journey

Paul's second missionary journey, which took place around 49-52 C.E., was marked by significant expansion of the Christian mission, the establishment of new churches, and deepening of existing ones. This journey also included important developments such as the introduction of the Gospel to Europe. This chapter provides a comprehensive account of Paul's second missionary journey, detailing key events, encounters, and the impact of his ministry.

The Disagreement and New Companions

The second journey began with a disagreement between Paul and Barnabas over whether to take John Mark with them. This disagreement led to their separation, with Barnabas taking John Mark to Cyprus and Paul choosing Silas as his new companion.

Acts 15:36-40 (UASV): "And after some days Paul said to Barnabas, 'Let us return and visit the brothers in every city where we proclaimed the word of the Lord, and see how they are.' Now Barnabas wanted to take with them John called Mark. But Paul thought best not to take with them one who had withdrawn from them in Pamphylia and had not gone with them to the work. And there arose a sharp disagreement, so that they separated from each other. Barnabas took Mark with him and sailed away to Cyprus, but Paul chose Silas and departed, having been commended by the brothers to the grace of the Lord."

Revisiting and Strengthening the Churches

Paul and Silas revisited the churches established during the first journey, strengthening the disciples and delivering the decisions of the Jerusalem Council, which had addressed issues concerning Gentile believers.

Acts 16:4-5 (UASV): "As they went on their way through the cities, they delivered to them for observance the decisions that had been reached by the apostles and elders who were in Jerusalem. So the churches were strengthened in the faith, and they increased in numbers daily."

Adding Timothy to the Team

In Lystra, Paul encountered Timothy, a young disciple well spoken of by the believers. Paul decided to take Timothy along, recognizing his potential for ministry. To avoid potential obstacles in their mission among Jews, Paul had Timothy circumcised.

Acts 16:1-3 (UASV): "Paul came also to Derbe and to Lystra. A disciple was there, named Timothy, the son of a Jewish woman who was a believer, but his father was a Greek. He was well spoken of by the brothers at Lystra and Iconium. Paul wanted Timothy to accompany him, and he took him and circumcised him because of the Jews who were in those places, for they all knew that his father was a Greek."

The Macedonian Call

The journey took a significant turn when Paul received a vision of a man from Macedonia pleading for help. Interpreting this vision as a divine directive, Paul and his companions set sail for Macedonia, marking the first time the Gospel would be preached in Europe.

Acts 16:9-10 (UASV): "And a vision appeared to Paul in the night: a man of Macedonia was standing there, urging him and saying, 'Come over to Macedonia and help us.' And when Paul had seen the vision, immediately we sought to go on into Macedonia, concluding that God had called us to preach the gospel to them."

Philippi: The Conversion of Lydia and the Philippian Jailer

In Philippi, Paul and Silas first preached the Gospel to a group of women gathered by a riverside. Among them was Lydia, a seller of purple goods, who became the first convert in Europe. Her home subsequently became a meeting place for believers.

Acts 16:14-15 (UASV): "One who heard us was a woman named Lydia, from the city of Thyatira, a seller of purple goods, who was a worshiper of God. The Lord opened her heart to pay attention to what was said by Paul. And after she was baptized, and her household as well, she urged us, saying, 'If you have judged me to be faithful to the Lord, come to my house and stay.' And she prevailed upon us."

Paul and Silas encountered opposition when they cast out a spirit of divination from a slave girl, causing economic loss to her owners. This led to their imprisonment. However, their prayers and hymns in prison resulted in a miraculous earthquake that opened the prison doors. The Philippian jailer, witnessing this, asked how he could be saved, leading to his and his household's conversion.

Acts 16:30-34 (UASV): "Then he brought them out and said, 'Sirs, what must I do to be saved?' And they said, 'Believe in the Lord Jesus, and you will be saved, you and your household.' And they spoke the word of the Lord to him and to all who were in his house. And he took them the same hour of the night and washed their wounds; and he was baptized at once, he and all his family. Then he brought them up into his house and set food before them. And he rejoiced along with his entire household that he had believed in God."

Thessalonica and Berea: Preaching and Opposition

Paul and Silas then traveled to Thessalonica, where they preached in the synagogue. Many Jews and God-fearing Greeks were persuaded, but opposition arose, leading to an uproar in the city. To protect Paul and Silas, the believers sent them away to Berea.

Acts 17:1-5 (UASV): "Now when they had passed through Amphipolis and Apollonia, they came to Thessalonica, where there was a synagogue of the Jews. And Paul went in, as was his custom, and on three Sabbath days he reasoned with them from the Scriptures, explaining and proving that it was necessary for the Christ to suffer and to rise from the dead, and saying, 'This Jesus, whom I proclaim to you, is the Christ.' And some of them were persuaded and joined Paul and Silas, as did a great many of the devout Greeks and not a few of the leading women. But the Jews were jealous, and taking some wicked men of the rabble, they formed a mob, set the city in an uproar, and attacked the house of Jason, seeking to bring them out to the crowd."

In Berea, the response to the Gospel was more favorable. The Bereans were noted for their noble character, as they examined the Scriptures daily to see if Paul's teachings were true. However, agitators from Thessalonica soon arrived, stirring up trouble once again.

Acts 17:11-12 (UASV): "Now these Jews were more noble than those in Thessalonica; they received the word with all eagerness, examining the Scriptures daily to see if these things were so. Many of them therefore believed, with not a few Greek women of high standing as well as men."

Athens: Engaging the Philosophers

Paul's journey continued to Athens, a city renowned for its philosophical schools and religious pluralism. Here, Paul delivered his famous speech at the Areopagus, addressing the Athenian philosophers and presenting the Gospel in terms they could understand.

Acts 17:22-23 (UASV): "So Paul, standing in the midst of the Areopagus, said: 'Men of Athens, I perceive that in every way you are very religious. For as I passed along and observed the objects of your worship, I found also an altar with this inscription, "To the unknown god." What therefore you worship as unknown, this I proclaim to you.'"

Paul's address focused on the nature of God as Creator, the call to repentance, and the resurrection of Jesus. While some mocked, others were intrigued, and a few believed, including Dionysius the Areopagite and a woman named Damaris.

Acts 17:32-34 (UASV): "Now when they heard of the resurrection of the dead, some mocked. But others said, 'We will hear you again about this.' So Paul went out from their midst. But some men joined him and believed, among whom also were Dionysius the Areopagite and a woman named Damaris and others with them."

Corinth: A Prolonged Ministry

Paul then traveled to Corinth, a major commercial hub with a reputation for moral laxity. Here, he met Aquila and Priscilla, fellow tentmakers who became important co-workers in his ministry. Paul stayed in Corinth for 18 months, preaching the Gospel and establishing a strong church.

Acts 18:1-3 (UASV): "After this Paul left Athens and went to Corinth. And he found a Jew named Aquila, a native of Pontus, recently come from Italy with his wife Priscilla, because Claudius had commanded all the Jews to leave Rome. And he went to see them, and because he was of the same trade he stayed with them and worked, for they were tentmakers by trade."

Despite opposition from some Jews, Paul's ministry in Corinth flourished, supported by a vision from the Lord encouraging him to continue his work there.

Acts 18:9-11 (UASV): "And the Lord said to Paul one night in a vision, 'Do not be afraid, but go on speaking and do not be silent, for I am with you, and no one will attack you to harm you, for I have many in this city who are my people.' And he stayed a year and six months, teaching the word of God among them."

Return to Antioch

After leaving Corinth, Paul made a brief stop in Ephesus, where he promised to return if God willed. He then sailed to Caesarea, greeted the church there, and finally returned to Antioch, completing his second missionary journey.

Acts 18:18-22 (UASV): "After this, Paul stayed many days longer and then took leave of the brothers and set sail for Syria, and with him Priscilla and Aquila. At Cenchreae he had cut his hair, for he was under a vow. And they came to Ephesus, and he left them there, but he himself went into the synagogue and reasoned with the Jews. When they asked him to stay for a longer period, he declined. But on taking leave of them he said, 'I will return to you if God wills,' and he set sail from Ephesus. When he had landed at Caesarea, he went up and greeted the church, and then went down to Antioch."

Paul's second missionary journey was a period of significant growth and expansion for the early church. It saw the establishment of new churches in Europe, the strengthening of existing ones, and the deepening of Paul's relationships with his fellow workers. This journey also highlighted the importance of resilience, adaptability, and reliance on God's guidance in the face of opposition and challenges. As Paul continued to spread the Gospel, his efforts laid a solid foundation for the continued growth of the Christian faith.

Chapter 18: Paul's Third Missionary Journey

Paul's third missionary journey, which took place around 53-57 C.E., was characterized by further strengthening of the churches, extensive teaching, and deepening theological reflection. This journey focused on revisiting established churches, expanding the mission, and solidifying the foundations of Christian communities. This chapter provides a detailed account of Paul's third missionary journey, highlighting key events, teachings, and the enduring impact of his ministry.

Revisiting Galatia and Phrygia

Paul began his third journey by traveling through the regions of Galatia and Phrygia, strengthening the disciples and encouraging the churches he had previously established. This focus on revisiting and fortifying existing communities underscores Paul's commitment to nurturing and supporting the fledgling Christian groups.

Acts 18:23 (UASV): "After spending some time there, he departed and went from one place to the next through the region of Galatia and Phrygia, strengthening all the disciples."

The Extended Stay in Ephesus

Ephesus became the central hub of Paul's third journey. He spent about three years in this influential city, which was a major center of commerce and pagan worship. Paul's ministry in Ephesus was marked by powerful preaching, miracles, and significant opposition.

Acts 19:1-7 (UASV): "And it happened that while Apollos was at Corinth, Paul passed through the inland country and came to Ephesus. There he found some disciples. And he said to them, 'Did you receive the Holy Spirit when you believed?' And they said, 'No, we have not even heard that there is a Holy Spirit.' And he said, 'Into what then were you baptized?' They said, 'Into John's baptism.' And Paul said,

'John baptized with the baptism of repentance, telling the people to believe in the one who was to come after him, that is, Jesus.' On hearing this, they were baptized in the name of the Lord Jesus. And when Paul had laid his hands on them, the Holy Spirit came on them, and they began speaking in tongues and prophesying. There were about twelve men in all."

Paul's teaching in the lecture hall of Tyrannus allowed him to reach a wide audience over two years, spreading the Gospel throughout the province of Asia.

Acts 19:8-10 (UASV): "And he entered the synagogue and for three months spoke boldly, reasoning and persuading them about the kingdom of God. But when some became stubborn and continued in unbelief, speaking evil of the Way before the congregation, he withdrew from them and took the disciples with him, reasoning daily in the hall of Tyrannus. This continued for two years, so that all the residents of Asia heard the word of the Lord, both Jews and Greeks."

Miracles and Opposition

Paul's time in Ephesus was marked by extraordinary miracles, which served to authenticate his apostolic ministry and the message of the Gospel.

Acts 19:11-12 (UASV): "And God was doing extraordinary miracles by the hands of Paul, so that even handkerchiefs or aprons that had touched his skin were carried away to the sick, and their diseases left them and the evil spirits came out of them."

However, his success also led to significant opposition. A notable instance involved a silversmith named Demetrius, whose business of making silver shrines of the goddess Artemis was threatened by Paul's teaching. This opposition culminated in a riot in Ephesus.

Acts 19:23-27 (UASV): "About that time there arose no little disturbance concerning the Way. For a man named Demetrius, a silversmith who made silver shrines of Artemis, brought no little business to the craftsmen. These he gathered together, with the workmen in similar trades, and said, 'Men, you know that from this business we have our wealth. And you see and hear that not only in Ephesus but in almost all of Asia this Paul has persuaded and turned away a great many people, saying that gods made with hands are not gods. And there is danger not only that this trade of ours may come into disrepute but also that the temple of the great goddess Artemis may be counted as nothing, and that she may even be deposed from her magnificence, she whom all Asia and the world worship.'"

Encouragement and Exhortation in Macedonia and Greece

After the tumult in Ephesus, Paul traveled through Macedonia, encouraging the believers and giving them much exhortation. He continued to strengthen the churches he had previously established.

Acts 20:1-2 (UASV): "After the uproar ceased, Paul sent for the disciples, and after encouraging them, he said farewell and departed for Macedonia. When he had gone through those regions and had given them much encouragement, he came to Greece."

During his stay in Greece, Paul likely wrote his Epistle to the Romans, a significant theological work that outlined the foundations of Christian doctrine.

Return to Troas: Eutychus Revived

Paul's journey back to Jerusalem included a notable stop in Troas, where he performed a miracle by reviving Eutychus, a young man who had fallen asleep and died after falling from a third-story window during Paul's extended teaching.

Acts 20:9-12 (UASV): "And a young man named Eutychus, sitting at the window, sank into a deep sleep as Paul talked still longer. And being overcome by sleep, he fell down from the third story and was taken up dead. But Paul went down and bent over him, and taking him in his arms, said, 'Do not be alarmed, for his life is in him.' And when Paul had gone up and had broken bread and eaten, he conversed with them a long while, until daybreak, and so departed. And they took the youth away alive, and were not a little comforted."

Farewell to the Ephesian Elders

On his way to Jerusalem, Paul called for the elders of the Ephesian church to meet him in Miletus. In a heartfelt farewell address, Paul recounted his ministry among them, warned them of future challenges, and charged them to be vigilant shepherds of the flock.

Acts 20:17-21 (UASV): "Now from Miletus he sent to Ephesus and called the elders of the church to come to him. And when they came to him, he said to them: 'You yourselves know how I lived among you the whole time from the first day that I set foot in Asia, serving the Lord with all humility and with tears and with trials that happened to me through the plots of the Jews; how I did not shrink from declaring to you anything that was profitable, and teaching you in public and from house to house, testifying both to Jews and to Greeks of repentance toward God and of faith in our Lord Jesus Christ.'"

Paul's address emphasized the need for vigilance and faithfulness, both in doctrine and practice. He expressed his commitment to the Gospel, regardless of the personal cost, and entrusted the church leaders to God's care.

Acts 20:28-31 (UASV): "Pay careful attention to yourselves and to all the flock, in which the Holy Spirit has made you overseers, to care for the church of God, which he obtained with his own blood. I know that after my departure fierce wolves will come in among you, not sparing the flock; and from among your own selves will arise men speaking twisted things, to draw away the disciples after them. Therefore be alert, remembering that for three years I did not cease night or day to admonish everyone with tears."

Journey to Jerusalem: Prophecies and Warnings

As Paul journeyed towards Jerusalem, he received multiple warnings from fellow believers about the dangers awaiting him. Despite these warnings, Paul remained resolute in his mission, demonstrating his unwavering commitment to God's call.

Acts 21:10-14 (UASV): "While we were staying for many days, a prophet named Agabus came down from Judea. And coming to us, he took Paul's belt and bound his own feet and hands and said, 'Thus says the Holy Spirit, "This is how the Jews at Jerusalem will bind the man who owns this belt and deliver him into the hands of the Gentiles."' When we heard this, we and the people there urged him not to go up to Jerusalem. Then Paul answered, 'What are you doing, weeping and breaking my heart? For I am ready not only to be imprisoned but even to die in Jerusalem for the name of the Lord Jesus.' And since he would not be persuaded, we ceased and said, 'Let the will of the Lord be done.'"

Arrival in Jerusalem

Paul's arrival in Jerusalem marked the culmination of his third missionary journey. Despite the warnings and the potential dangers, he was determined to deliver the collection for the poor and to strengthen the unity between the Gentile and Jewish believers.

Acts 21:17-19 (UASV): "When we had come to Jerusalem, the brothers received us gladly. On the following day Paul went in with us to James, and all the elders were present. After greeting them, he related one by one the things that God had done among the Gentiles through his ministry."

Paul's third missionary journey was a period of intense ministry, theological development, and significant growth for the early church. His work in Ephesus, the establishment of churches throughout Asia Minor, and his theological reflections in his letters left a lasting legacy. This journey also underscored the challenges and opposition that accompanied the spread of the Gospel, highlighting the need for resilience, faith, and reliance on God's guidance. Through his unwavering commitment and tireless efforts, Paul laid the groundwork for the continued expansion and strengthening of the Christian faith.

Chapter 19: Paul's Arrest, First, and Second Imprisonments at Rome

Paul's arrest and subsequent imprisonments in Rome are pivotal events in his life and ministry. These periods of confinement provided unique opportunities for Paul to witness to the Roman authorities, to write several of his epistles, and to continue influencing the early Christian church despite his physical limitations. This chapter examines the circumstances of Paul's arrest, his first and second imprisonments, and the significant lessons and contributions from these challenging periods.

Arrest in Jerusalem

Paul's arrest occurred shortly after his arrival in Jerusalem, following his third missionary journey. Despite warnings from fellow believers about the dangers that awaited him, Paul was resolute in his mission to deliver the collection for the poor and to bridge the gap between Jewish and Gentile believers. His presence in the temple led to accusations from some Jews who alleged that he had brought Gentiles into the temple, thereby defiling it.

Acts 21:27-30 (UASV): "When the seven days were almost completed, the Jews from Asia, seeing him in the temple, stirred up the whole crowd and laid hands on him, crying out, 'Men of Israel, help! This is the man who is teaching everyone everywhere against the people and the law and this place. Moreover, he even brought Greeks into the temple and has defiled this holy place.' For they had previously seen Trophimus the Ephesian with him in the city, and they supposed that Paul had brought him into the temple. Then all the city was stirred up, and the people ran together. They seized Paul and dragged him out of the temple, and at once the gates were shut."

Imprisonment in Caesarea

Following his arrest, Paul was taken into Roman custody to protect him from the mob. He was subsequently transferred to Caesarea, where he remained imprisoned for two years. During this time, Paul had several hearings before Roman governors Felix and Festus, as well as an audience with King Agrippa.

Acts 24:24-27 (UASV): "After some days Felix came with his wife Drusilla, who was Jewish, and he sent for Paul and heard him speak about faith in Christ Jesus. And as he reasoned about righteousness and self-control and the coming judgment, Felix was alarmed and said, 'Go away for the present. When I get an opportunity I will summon you.' At the same time he hoped that money would be given him by Paul. So he sent for him often and conversed with him. When two years had elapsed, Felix was succeeded by Porcius Festus. And desiring to do the Jews a favor, Felix left Paul in prison."

During these hearings, Paul consistently defended his faith and proclaimed the Gospel, demonstrating his unwavering commitment to his mission despite his imprisonment.

Journey to Rome

Paul's appeal to Caesar led to his transfer to Rome, a journey fraught with challenges, including a shipwreck on the island of Malta. Despite these difficulties, Paul continued to witness to those around him, including the ship's crew and the inhabitants of Malta.

Acts 27:23-24 (UASV): "For this very night there stood before me an angel of the God to whom I belong and whom I worship, and he said, 'Do not be afraid, Paul; you must stand before Caesar. And behold, God has granted you all those who sail with you.'"

Acts 28:7-9 (UASV): "Now in the neighborhood of that place were lands belonging to the chief man of the island, named Publius, who received us and entertained us hospitably for three days. It happened that the father of Publius lay sick with fever and dysentery. And Paul visited him and prayed, and putting his hands on him healed him. And when this had taken place, the rest of the people on the island who had diseases also came and were cured."

First Imprisonment in Rome

Upon his arrival in Rome, Paul was placed under house arrest, living in a rented house where he was free to receive visitors and continue his ministry. During this period, Paul wrote several of his epistles, including Ephesians, Philippians, Colossians, and Philemon.

Acts 28:30-31 (UASV): "He lived there two whole years at his own expense, and welcomed all who came to him, proclaiming the kingdom of God and teaching about the Lord Jesus Christ with all boldness and without hindrance."

Paul's letters from this period reflect his deep theological insights and pastoral concerns. In Ephesians, he elaborates on the mystery of Christ and the unity of the church. In Philippians, he expresses joy and encouragement despite his circumstances. Colossians emphasizes the supremacy of Christ, and Philemon addresses the issue of Christian brotherhood and forgiveness.

Release and Further Ministry

There is evidence to suggest that Paul was released after his first imprisonment and continued his missionary work, possibly traveling to Spain as he had expressed a desire to do so in his letter to the Romans.

Romans 15:24 (UASV): "I hope to see you in passing as I go to Spain, and to be helped on my journey there by you, once I have enjoyed your company for a while."

During this period of freedom, Paul likely wrote the pastoral epistles—1 Timothy and Titus—providing guidance for church leaders and addressing issues of church organization and doctrine.

Second Imprisonment in Rome

Paul's second imprisonment in Rome was markedly different from his first. This time, he was likely held in harsher conditions, possibly in the Mamertine Prison. It was during this imprisonment that Paul wrote his second letter to Timothy, which reflects a somber tone and a sense of impending martyrdom.

2 Timothy 1:16-18 (UASV): "May the Lord grant mercy to the household of Onesiphorus, for he often refreshed me and was not ashamed of my chains, but when he arrived in Rome he searched for me earnestly and found me—may the Lord grant him to find mercy from the Lord on that Day!—and you well know all the service he rendered at Ephesus."

In this letter, Paul expresses his loneliness and the desertion of some of his companions, but also his unwavering faith and hope in Christ.

2 Timothy 4:6-8 (UASV): "For I am already being poured out as a drink offering, and the time of my departure has come. I have fought the good fight, I have finished the race, I have kept the faith. Henceforth there is laid up for me the crown of righteousness, which the Lord, the righteous judge, will award to me on that Day, and not only to me but also to all who have loved his appearing."

Martyrdom and Legacy

Tradition holds that Paul was martyred under the Roman Emperor Nero, around 64-67 C.E. He was likely beheaded, a fate reserved for Roman citizens. Paul's willingness to suffer and die for the sake of the Gospel underscores his profound commitment to Christ and his mission.

Paul's imprisonments and ultimate martyrdom left an indelible mark on the early Christian church. His letters, written during these times of confinement, continue to inspire and instruct believers to this day. His example of steadfast faith in the face of persecution and his theological insights have profoundly shaped Christian doctrine and practice.

Lessons from Paul's Imprisonments

1. **Faithfulness in Adversity**: Paul's example teaches us to remain faithful to our calling despite hardships. His ability to continue ministering and writing during his imprisonments shows that God can use us in any circumstance.

2. **The Power of Prayer and Encouragement**: Paul's letters often include prayers and words of encouragement, highlighting the importance of supporting one another in the faith.

3. **The Sovereignty of God**: Paul's experiences underscore the belief that God is sovereign and can bring about His purposes even through difficult and seemingly negative situations.

4. **The Importance of Doctrine**: Paul's epistles, written during his imprisonments, contain rich theological content that is foundational to Christian belief and practice. This underscores the importance of sound doctrine and teaching in the life of the church.

By reflecting on Paul's imprisonments, we can draw strength and inspiration for our own faith journeys, learning to trust in God's sovereignty, remain faithful in adversity, and continue to support and encourage one another in the body of Christ.

Chapter 20: Paul: An Example Worthy of Imitation

The apostle Paul stands as a towering figure in Christian history, not only for his theological contributions and missionary zeal but also for his exemplary life of faith, dedication, and endurance. Paul's life and ministry offer rich lessons for believers, highlighting the virtues of humility, perseverance, love, and unwavering commitment to Christ. This chapter explores how Paul's example is worthy of imitation, drawing insights from his teachings, actions, and personal experiences.

Humility and Service

Paul's life was characterized by profound humility and a servant's heart. Despite his significant role and numerous accomplishments, Paul consistently attributed his success to God's grace and power rather than his own abilities.

1 Corinthians 15:9-10 (UASV): "For I am the least of the apostles, unworthy to be called an apostle, because I persecuted the church of God. But by the grace of God I am what I am, and his grace toward me was not in vain. On the contrary, I worked harder than any of them, though it was not I, but the grace of God that is with me."

Paul's humility is further exemplified in his willingness to serve others selflessly, often putting their needs above his own. He labored tirelessly to support himself financially to avoid being a burden to the churches he served.

Acts 20:33-35 (UASV): "I coveted no one's silver or gold or apparel. You yourselves know that these hands ministered to my necessities and to those who were with me. In all things I have shown you that by working hard in this way we must help the weak and remember the words of the Lord Jesus, how he himself said, 'It is more blessed to give than to receive.'"

Perseverance in Suffering

Paul's life was marked by intense suffering and persecution, yet he remained steadfast in his faith and mission. His perseverance through trials serves as a powerful example for believers facing their own challenges.

2 Corinthians 11:23-28 (UASV): "Are they servants of Christ? I am a better one—I am talking like a madman—with far greater labors, far more imprisonments, with countless beatings, and often near death. Five times I received at the hands of the Jews the forty lashes less one. Three times I was beaten with rods. Once I was stoned. Three times I was shipwrecked; a night and a day I was adrift at sea; on frequent journeys, in danger from rivers, danger from robbers, danger from my own people, danger from Gentiles, danger in the city, danger in the wilderness, danger at sea, danger from false brothers; in toil and hardship, through many a sleepless night, in hunger and thirst, often without food, in cold and exposure. And, apart from other things, there is the daily pressure on me of my anxiety for all the churches."

Paul's endurance was rooted in his unwavering trust in God's sovereignty and his eternal perspective on life. He viewed his sufferings as momentary afflictions in light of the eternal glory awaiting him.

Romans 8:18 (UASV): "For I consider that the sufferings of this present time are not worth comparing with the glory that is to be revealed to us."

Passion for the Gospel

Paul's passion for the Gospel and his unwavering commitment to proclaiming the message of Christ were evident throughout his life. He tirelessly preached the Gospel, planted churches, and wrote letters to instruct and encourage believers.

Romans 1:16 (UASV): "For I am not ashamed of the gospel, for it is the power of God for salvation to everyone who believes, to the Jew first and also to the Greek."

Paul's zeal for the Gospel was driven by his profound love for Christ and his desire to see others come to faith. His missionary journeys, letters, and personal sacrifices all reflect his dedication to the cause of Christ.

1 Corinthians 9:19-23 (UASV): "For though I am free from all, I have made myself a servant to all, that I might win more of them. To the Jews I became as a Jew, in order to win Jews. To those under the law I became as one under the law (though not being myself under the law) that I might win those under the law. To those outside the law I became as one outside the law (not being outside the law of God but under the law of Christ) that I might win those outside the law. To the weak I became weak, that I might win the weak. I have become all things to all people, that by all means I might save some. I do it all for the sake of the gospel, that I may share with them in its blessings."

Commitment to Discipleship

Paul's commitment to discipleship is evident in his relationships with individuals such as Timothy, Titus, and many others. He invested in their lives, providing instruction, encouragement, and correction to help them grow in their faith and ministry.

2 Timothy 2:1-2 (UASV): "You then, my child, be strengthened by the grace that is in Christ Jesus, and what you have heard from me in the presence of many witnesses entrust to faithful men who will be able to teach others also."

Paul's letters to Timothy and Titus, known as the Pastoral Epistles, are filled with practical guidance for church leadership and personal conduct, reflecting his dedication to preparing the next generation of leaders.

Love and Compassion

Paul's letters often convey his deep love and compassion for the believers he ministered to. He viewed himself as a spiritual father to many, caring deeply for their spiritual well-being and rejoicing in their growth.

1 Thessalonians 2:7-8 (UASV): "But we were gentle among you, like a nursing mother taking care of her own children. So, being affectionately desirous of you, we were ready to share with you not only the gospel of God but also our own selves, because you had become very dear to us."

Paul's love for the churches is also evident in his willingness to address difficult issues, offering correction and guidance with the goal of building them up in faith and unity.

Ephesians 4:1-3 (UASV): "I therefore, a prisoner for the Lord, urge you to walk in a manner worthy of the calling to which you have been called, with all humility and gentleness, with patience, bearing with one another in love, eager to maintain the unity of the Spirit in the bond of peace."

Faith and Hope

Paul's faith and hope in Christ were the foundation of his life and ministry. He constantly encouraged believers to stand firm in their faith and to keep their eyes fixed on the hope of eternal life.

Philippians 3:13-14 (UASV): "Brothers, I do not consider that I have made it my own. But one thing I do: forgetting what lies behind and straining forward to what lies ahead, I press on toward the goal for the prize of the upward call of God in Christ Jesus."

Paul's letters are filled with expressions of his confident hope in God's promises and his assurance of salvation. This hope sustained him through trials and motivated him to persevere in his mission.

Romans 8:38-39 (UASV): "For I am sure that neither death nor life, nor angels nor rulers, nor things present nor things to come, nor powers, nor height nor depth, nor anything else in all creation, will be able to separate us from the love of God in Christ Jesus our Lord."

Paul's Call to Imitation

Paul frequently encouraged believers to imitate him as he imitated Christ. He recognized that his life was a tangible example of living out the principles of the Gospel, and he sought to model this for others.

1 Corinthians 11:1 (UASV): "Be imitators of me, as I am of Christ."

Philippians 3:17 (UASV): "Brothers, join in imitating me, and keep your eyes on those who walk according to the example you have in us."

Paul's call to imitation underscores the importance of living a life that reflects the values and teachings of Christ. By following Paul's example, believers can learn to navigate the challenges of life with faith, love, and unwavering commitment to the Gospel.

Conclusion: Paul's Enduring Legacy

The life and ministry of the apostle Paul provide a powerful example of what it means to live a life fully devoted to Christ. His humility, perseverance, passion for the Gospel, commitment to discipleship, love, and faith offer valuable lessons for believers today. By studying and emulating Paul's example, we can grow in our own faith and contribute to the ongoing mission of the church.

Paul's legacy continues to inspire and challenge believers to live lives worthy of the calling they have received. His writings remain foundational to Christian theology and practice, and his life serves as a testament to the transformative power of the Gospel. As we seek to follow Paul's example, we are reminded of the words he wrote to the Corinthians:

1 Corinthians 15:58 (UASV): "Therefore, my beloved brothers, be steadfast, immovable, always abounding in the work of the Lord, knowing that in the Lord your labor is not in vain."

Bibliography

Aldrich, C. J. (1981). *Lifestyle Evangelism*. Portland, OR: Multnoma Press.

Andrews, E. D. (2016). *THE CHRISTIAN APOLOGIST: Always Being Prepared to Make a Defense [Second Edition]*. Cambridge, OH: Christian Publishing House.

Andrews, E. D. (2016). *THE EVANGELISM HANDBOOK: How All Christians Can Effectively Share God's Word in Their Community, [SECOND EDITION]*. Cambridge, OH: Christian Publishing House.

Andrews, E. D. (2017). *CONVERSATIONAL EVANGELISM: Defending the Faith, Reasoning from the Scriptures, Explaining and Proving, Instructing in Sound Doctrine, and Overturning False Reasoning [Second Edition]*. Cambridge, OH: Christian Publishing House.

Andrews, E. D. (2018). *CHRISTIAN APOLOGETIC EVANGELISM: Reaching Hearts with the Art of Persuasion*. Cambridge, OH: Christian Publishing House.

Andrews, E. D. (2018). *REASONING WITH THE WORLD'S VARIOUS RELIGIONS: Examining and Evangelizing Other Faiths*. Cambridge, OH: Christian Publishing House.

Andrews, E. D., & Overton, T. (2018). *THE GREAT TEACHER JESUS CHRIST: What Made Jesus Christ's Teaching, Preaching, Evangelism, and Apologetics Outstandingly Effective?* Cambridge, OH: Christian Publishing House.

Bechtle, D. M. (2006). *Evangelism for the Rest of Us: Sharing Christ within Your Personality Style*. Grand Rapids, MI: Baker Books.

Boa, K., & Kruidenier, W. (2000). *Holman New Testament Commentary: Romans*. Nashville: Broadman & Holman.

Caba, T. e. (2007). *The Apologetics Study Bible: Real Questions, Straight Answers, Stronger Faith*. Nashville: Holman Bible Publishers.

Coleman, R. E. (2010). *The Master Plan of Evangelism*. Grand Rapids, MI: Revell.

Geisler, D. a. (2009, 2014). *Conversational Evangelism.* EUGENE, OREGON: Harvest House Publishers.

Green, M. (2004). *Evangelism in the Early Church.* Grand Rapids, MI: Eerdmans.

MacArthur, J. F. (2011). *Evangelism: How to Share the Gospel Faithfully (MacArthur Pastor's Library).* Nashville, TN: Thomas Nelson.

McRaney, W. (2003). *The Art of Personal Evangelism.* Nashville: Broadman & Holman.

McRaney, W. (2003). *The Art of Personal Evangelism: Sharing Jesus in a Changing Culture.* Grand Rapids, MI: B&H Academic.

Reid, A. (2009). *Evangelism Handbook: Biblical, Spiritual, Intentional, Missional.* Grand Rapids, MI: B&H Academic.

Reid, A. (2017). *Sharing Jesus without Freaking Out: Evangelism the Way You Were Born to Do It.* Grand Rapid, MI: B&H Academic.

Stiles, J. M. (2014). *Evangelism: How the Whole Church Speaks of Jesus (9marks: Building Healthy Churches).* Wheaton, IL: Crossway.

Story, D. (1999). *Engaging the Closed Minded: Presenting Your Faith to the Confirmed Unbeliever.* Grand Rapids, MI: Kregel Publications.

www.ingramcontent.com/pod-product-compliance
Lightning Source LLC
Chambersburg PA
CBHW022107040426
42451CB00007B/163